T0005995

THE
BLACK
BRITISH
QUIZ BOOK

THE
BLACK
BRITISH
QUIZ BOOK

The UK's largest
Black British pub quiz

PRTYHERE

HarperCollins*Publishers*

HarperCollins*Publishers*
1 London Bridge Street
London SE1 9GF

www.harpercollins.co.uk

HarperCollins*Publishers*
Macken House, 39/40 Mayor Street Upper
Dublin 1, D01 C9W8, Ireland

First published by HarperCollins*Publishers* 2023

10 9 8 7 6 5 4 3 2 1

A catalogue record of this book is available from the British Library

ISBN 978-0-00-858431-3

Printed and bound in the UK using 100% renewable electricity at
CPI Group (UK) Ltd

MIX
Paper | Supporting
responsible forestry
FSC
www.fsc.org   **FSC™ C007454**

This book is produced from independently certified FSC™ paper to ensure
responsible forest management.

For more information visit: www.harpercollins.co.uk/green

CONTENTS

Introduction		1
1	NOT-SO-GENERAL KNOWLEDGE	5
2	ARE YOU SMARTER THAN A 10-YEAR-OLD?	67
3	A QUESTION OF SPORT	81
4	MUSIC	109
	Guess the song	111
	UK garage	115
	Grime	116
5	CULTURE	117
	Pop culture	119
	Film and TV	120
	Anime	124
	Marvel	125
	Fashion	126
	Who am I?	128
	Twitter and TikTok	132
	My Wife and Kids	134
6	HISTORY	135
	Black history	137
	1980s	153
	1990s	154

	2000s	156
	2010s	161
7	GEOGRAPHY	163
8	POLITICS	191
9	FOOD AND DRINK	195
10	EVENTS	201
11	MERRY QUIZMAS!	205
12	PUZZLES	209
	Anagrams	211
	Fill in the blanks	222
	Word search	223
	Map of the world	226
ANSWERS		227
Acknowledgements		314

INTRODUCTION

PRTYHERE is home to the UK's largest Black British pub quiz night. PRTYHERE started when two friends grew frustrated with the lack of diversity when it came to casual nights out in London. Well, the actual idea came from when one of us went to a pub quiz and couldn't answer a single question . . . We realised pub quizzes were completely culturally specific and by their nature a reflection of the people writing the questions!

This quiz book is written by two Black British women for Black British people and, at the time we're writing this, is the first ever quiz book that centres on the Black British community. This is not to say that it can't be enjoyed by all, but expect questions pertaining to Black culture across all its facets – and broader questions too.

Inside you'll find over 2,500 questions across a range of different topics, from sport to anime, geography to TikTok, Channel U to Windrush and more.

We've loved writing these quizzes for *you* and can't wait for you to use them to host your own quiz night with your loved ones.

Enjoy!

Sanae & Shay x

DISCLAIMER

This is by no means an exhaustive quiz book! The Black British community has a vast history and is creating new historic, hilarious and ground-breaking moments every day. As a result there will be many things not included in the book. If you think there might be multiple answers to a question – or if you're not sure that an answer is right – don't let it spoil the fun. Feel free to check it and replace it for your own quiz night – you are the quiz master now!

THE QUIZZES

The book is divided into quizzes on various topics and each round is usually made up of 15 questions. For the optimal experience we'd advise choosing between five and eight different rounds for your quiz and making sure you select your topics carefully with your audience in mind.

RUNNING A QUIZ

1. A good quiz master = a good quiz. Have a quick practice, know which rounds you're selecting in advance and have fun. Remember, whatever you say goes!
2. We've found that getting teams to use paper and pen feels very authentic, so make sure there's enough to go around. There should be one to two pieces of paper and one pen per team.

3. We recommend reading each question twice. The pace and timing of the quiz is completely up to you, but it's worth bearing in mind that people can get distracted if things take too long.
4. Ask everyone to put their phones away to ensure there's no cheating.
5. For the most part the quizzes are one point per answer, but half points or additional points can of course be awarded at the discretion of the quiz master.
6. You will find the answers at the back of this book. Read out the answers after every few rounds to keep up the momentum.
7. Prizes. No matter how big or small, everyone is in it for a prize, so make sure you let participants know what's on offer.

1

NOT-SO-GENERAL KNOWLEDGE

A PRTYHERE staple, this is one for our all-rounders, so in this round expect questions on anything and everything. The answers can be found on pages 227–255.

NOT-SO-GENERAL KNOWLEDGE

ROUND 1

1. Tope Awotona founded which tech company?
2. 'Anansi' is the name for which animal, referred to in African folklore tales?
3. What does ULEZ stand for?
4. Which British-Nigerian poet wrote 'Oil Music'?
5. In a game of poker, what is the second-strongest hand?
6. Who is Jermaine Sinclair Scott more commonly known as?
7. What colour is the shade myrtle?
8. Name the leading lady of So Solid Crew.
9. On which day of the year is Windrush Day celebrated in the UK?
10. What was the rapper Dave's character called in the hit TV show *Topboy*?
11. 'Pass that Dutch', 'Lose Control' and 'Work It' are hit singles from which artist?
12. Algophobia is the fear of what?
13. In December 1987, who became the first Black British woman to feature on the cover of *Vogue* magazine?
14. Name the common prefix that can mean 'crown', 'royalty' or 'wealth' in the Yoruba language.
15. Coldharbour Lane in London leads from Camberwell to which inner-city London district?

NOT-SO-GENERAL KNOWLEDGE

ROUND 2

1. Name the Muslim celebration that comes at the end of the holy month of Ramadan.
2. Which TV series featured Lakewood Elementary School?
3. Which 'W' is the pidgin English word for trouble?
4. Alongside Richard Curtis, who co-founded Comic Relief?
5. What year was Black History Month first celebrated in the UK?
6. Name the main villain in the 1973 James Bond film *Live and Let Die*.
7. What is the official currency in the Bahamas?
8. Name the first Afrobeat artist to sell out their show in Madison Square Garden, New York.
9. Name the first Black woman to be elected as a Member of Parliament in the UK.
10. What does OTF stand for?
11. Jamaican bun and cheese is traditionally eaten during which festive holiday?
12. Callaloo belongs to which food group?
13. The West African dish eba is made by adding boiling water to what?
14. Michael Ebenezer Kwadjo Omari Owuo Jr is more commonly known as who?
15. *Finding Me* is the memoir of which US actor?

NOT-SO-GENERAL KNOWLEDGE

ROUND 3

1. What the UK call 'aubergine', the US call what?
2. Name the woman known to many as the mother of the Notting Hill Carnival.
3. Name the Conservative politician who has previously served as Secretary of State for International Trade, President of the Board of Trade, and Minister for Women and Equalities.
4. In what year did the Biafra War start?
5. Name the traditional Moroccan cooking vessel used for slow-cooking meats and stews.
6. Randy, Cherise Roberts and Nadia Shepherd were all members of which group in the year 2000?
7. What represents the letter 'S' in the NATO phonetic alphabet?
8. Gerontology is the study of what?
9. Who was the first UK rapper to be signed to ROC nation?
10. Dollis Hill is in which London borough?
11. Metatarsalgia is the name for pain in which part of the body?
12. What is the main religion in Egypt?
13. What does the second 'A' in NAACP stand for?
14. Diane Parish plays which character in *EastEnders*?
15. What is the main ingredient in the dish kelewele?

NOT-SO-GENERAL KNOWLEDGE

ROUND 4

1. Léon-Mba Airport is located in which country?
2. The north London derby refers to which two teams playing against each other?
3. In which US district is Howard University based?
4. Gershom and Eliezer were the sons of who in the Bible?
5. Which nation is widely accepted as the birthplace of coffee?
6. Who is Ayodeji Ibrahim Balogun more commonly known as?
7. Espresso coffee liqueur and Irish cream in a shot glass make which drink?
8. What is the non-English language spoken by the majority of the Zimbabwean populace?
9. From which continent did the spice ginger originate?
10. Which type of blood cells does the disease sickle cell impact?
11. Which vegetable won the competition for outlasting the tenure of former prime minister Liz Truss?
12. Rose Hudson-Wilkin is the first Black British woman to become a what?
13. Which actor plays Ariel in the 2023 film *The Little Mermaid*?
14. Kente is the name for the fabric design popular in which country?
15. Which British-American author wrote the book *Ace of Spades*?

NOT-SO-GENERAL KNOWLEDGE

ROUND 5

1. Which is the most populous island in the West Indies?
2. What was the name of Skepta's first piece of artwork?
3. Referred to as 'Mean Girls Day', on which date did Kady ask Aaron Samuels what day it was?
4. In which square is the Ghanaian High Commission located in London?
5. The documentary *The Millionaire Preacher* was presented by who?
6. Berber people are the indigenous tribe of which region?
7. 'I'm rooting for everybody Black' was said in a red-carpet interview by who?
8. London City Airport is located in which borough?
9. The university-based game show *The Big Clash* was founded in what year?
10. What is the name for the head wrap worn mostly at weddings and celebratory events by Nigerian women?
11. Which actor played King Ghezo in the 2022 film *The Woman King*?
12. Name the market located in the centre of Dalston connecting Dalston Lane and Kingsland High Street.
13. Where was Usher at 7 o'clock?
14. What is the national dish of Jamaica?
15. Which American girl group were originally known as Girl's Tyme?

NOT-SO-GENERAL KNOWLEDGE

ROUND 6

1. The UK rap group Smoke Boys changed their name in 2018 from what?
2. Animals can be divided into five distinct groups: amphibians, reptiles, fish, birds and what?
3. Who played Aneka in the movie *Black Panther: Wakanda Forever*?
4. The United Kingdom, followed by Ireland, are the world's largest consumers of Guinness. Which country is third?
5. Alesha Dixon was a member of which early 2000s group?
6. In which country is Indomie manufactured?
7. If someone is gesticulating, what are they doing?
8. Pasteis de Nata is a custard tart dessert from which country?
9. Name one of the two areas of London in which the first Nando's restaurants in the UK opened.
10. In what year did it become illegal to smoke in certain public places in the UK?
11. Which flight is shorter, Birmingham to Amsterdam or Jamaica to Trinidad and Tobago?
12. Who wrote *The Brown Sisters* trilogy?
13. Mutya, Heidi, Siobhan and Keisha are the first names of members of which girl band?
14. According to Nigerian culture, it is frowned upon to eat, greet, collect or give things with your what?
15. Which artist created the drawing *The Scramble for Africa*?

NOT-SO-GENERAL KNOWLEDGE

ROUND 7

1. What were the last words said by Jesus in the Bible?
2. Who directed the five-part documentary *The Evolution of Black British Music* alongside Nicky 'Slimting' Walker?
3. Artist duo Lotto-Boyzz hail from which UK city?
4. The British producer Jonathan Kweku Awote-Mensah is better known as what?
5. Trevor Nelson began his career at which (originally pirate) radio station?
6. Name the band who headlined Glastonbury in 1999, making their lead singer Skin the first Black British female to do so.
7. British DJ and producer Andre Williams is better known by which stage name?
8. *Yinka, Where Is Your Huzband?* is written by which author?
9. Highlife is a style of music originating from which country?
10. Who wrote the book *Black and British*?
11. What is the measurement of the physical weight of diamonds?
12. Which entrepreneur is the host of the popular podcast *Diary of a CEO*?
13. Name the presenter most well known for their role on CBBC from 2000 to 2006, namely on *Xchange* and *50/50*.
14. The infamous Lawrence Anini of Benin City was known for committing which crime?
15. Who wrote the book *Why I'm No Longer Talking to White People About Race*?

NOT-SO-GENERAL KNOWLEDGE

ROUND 8

1. Album of the Year, Song of the Year, Record of the Year and which other award are known as the 'Big Four' at the Grammys?
2. In which decade was comedienne Gina Yashere born?
3. Which constituency did Paul Boateng represent?
4. In bingo, what number is represented by the phrase 'Two Little Ducks'?
5. Which group were featured on the remix of Stormzy's 2022 hit 'Hide & Seek'.
6. Who voices the characters of both Huey and Riley Freeman in the Boondocks?
7. In 2008, who was the first Black woman to walk in a Prada fashion show?
8. In what year did Rihanna join Matt Cardle as a guest appearance on *The X Factor* to perform 'Unfaithful'?
9. 'Way Down in the Hole' is the theme song to which hit TV show?
10. What is the third layer of the earth after the inner core and outer core?
11. Who sang the gospel song 'Never Would Have Made It'?
12. An old 'what's' tale is a generally accepted belief that is just based on superstition.
13. The names Kehinde and Taiwo in the Yoruba tradition signify what?
14. Koffi Olomidé is an artist originating from which country?
15. Who was the first prime minister of Jamaica?

NOT-SO-GENERAL KNOWLEDGE

ROUND 9

1. ByteDance is the parent company of which social media app?
2. Who had the 2010 hit 'Written in the Stars'?
3. Who made the viral freestyle to 'turn the cooker off, before you burn the jollof'.
4. Complete the phrase 'fine girl, no _____'.
5. Airline Ryanair has which two colours in its logo?
6. Launched in 2017, which restaurant pop-up became the first Black-owned brand to have a food stall in Selfridges?
7. What is located at 87–135 Brompton Road, London?
8. 'Allemagne' in French is the name of which country in English?
9. Name the clothing brand owned by British model Leomie Anderson.
10. Name the Chief Digital Officer at Microsoft who won the number 1 spot on the 2022 *Powerlist: Most Influential Black Britons*.
11. In what year did the Somali Civil War begin?
12. If Giggs has 'SN1 on his tee', what brand were his black trousers from?
13. What does cultural icon Irene Agbontaen's clothing brand TTYA stand for?
14. What do people with misophonia dislike?
15. What does HMRC stand for?

NOT-SO-GENERAL KNOWLEDGE

ROUND 10

1. Proverbially, a bird in the hand is worth two in the what?
2. 'If There's Any Justice', 'What About Love' and 'Time to Grow' were songs by which singer who came to fame through a reality show?
3. What does BIPOC stand for?
4. Chioma, Ngozi and Adaeze are names from which Nigerian ethnic group?
5. Ifemelu, Obinze, Dike and Aunty Uju are characters from which book?
6. Which comedian played shows in the *Back to Abnormal* tour?
7. Who played Lisa Wilkes in *The Fresh Prince of Bel-Air*?
8. Who was the voice of *Rastamouse*?
9. What is the largest landlocked country in South America?
10. What is the UK slang word meaning 'obvious' or 'suspicious'?
11. In what year did the Millennium Dome open?
12. If a clothing item has a circle inside a square, what does this mean?
13. What is the highest mountain in Africa?
14. The infamous Billy McFarland staged which festival?
15. Manchego, provolone and Asiago are all types of what?

NOT-SO-GENERAL KNOWLEDGE

ROUND 11

1. Name the premium spiced-rum brand whose name translates as 'The Waves'.
2. 'You think you hot, hot' is the opening line of the hit song 'Hot Hot' by which artist?
3. What is located at 20 Dean's Yard, London?
4. Who released the album *Tongue n' Cheek* in 2009?
5. The plural of which British first name is used in UK slang to refer to police officers?
6. Who released an album in 2001 titled *They Don't Know*?
7. What type of animal is Timon from *The Lion King*?
8. Which *Harry Potter* film is the fifth in the series?
9. In what year did the Battle of the Caribbean end?
10. LGA is the airport code for which US airport?
11. In what year did Giggs release 'Talkin' da Hardest'?
12. *Open Water* is a book written by which Black British author?
13. Complete the Nigerian proverb: The child of an elephant will not be a _____.
14. '"For I know the plans I have for you," declares the Lord, "plans to prosper you and not to harm you, plans to give you hope and a future."' Name the book, chapter and verse of the Bible that is this taken from.
15. What is the name given to a group of horses?

NOT-SO-GENERAL KNOWLEDGE

ROUND 12

1. Deities Shiva, Lakshmi and Hariti are all found in which religion?
2. What does GIF stand for?
3. What type of diving uses a self-contained underwater breathing apparatus?
4. What language is spoken in Denmark?
5. What is the name of the wife and mother in the TV show *Desmond's*?
6. In which season of the show *My Wife and Kids* did the actor playing Claire get replaced?
7. What are the two main characters' names in *Only Fools and Horses*.
8. 'I'm the captain now' is a line from which film?
9. The '2 for 2' deal was originally introduced by which British food chain?
10. Name the first book released by author Louise Rennison.
11. Who gave Princess Diana the name the 'People's Princess'?
12. Who was prime minister in 1991?
13. The African Union was created in what year?
14. Which celebrity housed Meghan Markle and Prince Harry?
15. Who wrote the song 'Black Boys'?

NOT-SO-GENERAL KNOWLEDGE

ROUND 13

1. Day-Date, Sea-Dweller and Milgauss are all models of what?
2. What is the newest country in Africa as of 2011?
3. What was the first drill song to go to Number 1 in the UK?
4. Which British territory in the Caribbean most recently gained independence?
5. What are the names of Jamie's brothers in *Top Boy*?
6. What is a Goliath birdeater?
7. Which comedian won *Britain's Got Talent* in 2022?
8. Name the frozen confectionery that consists of ice cream in a cup and a bubblegum ball at the bottom.
9. Ishmael and Isaac are sons of who in the Bible?
10. How many vowels are there in the Yoruba alphabet?
11. Sean Kingston's 'Beautiful Girls' samples which 1960s song?
12. Who attempted to blow up Parliament in 1605?
13. React, Python and Scala are examples of what?
14. What is the name of the pet cat in *Sabrina the Teenage Witch*?
15. Name the character who owned the Kwik-E-Mart in *The Simpsons*.

NOT-SO-GENERAL KNOWLEDGE

ROUND 14

1. In which London borough was the first Starbucks opened in the UK?
2. How many years of marriage would you have celebrated to reach your crystal anniversary?
3. Who, as of 2022, has the most liked photo on Instagram?
4. Name the BBC show based on the best-selling novel by criminal defence barrister Imran Mahmood.
5. In which month and year did the UK enter the second Covid lockdown?
6. In what year did Apple release the iPhone X?
7. Name the hunting dog originating in Africa that does not bark but yodels
8. A bananaquit is what type of creature?
9. Lake Killarney is a lake on which group of Caribbean islands?
10. Who plays Tracey Gordon in *Chewing Gum*?
11. What is the official currency of Iceland?
12. What is the more common name for the laryngeal prominence?
13. Which country has the internet domain .za?
14. 'Stand and Sing of _____, Proud and Free' is the national anthem of which country?
15. What is Frank Bowling's profession?

NOT-SO-GENERAL KNOWLEDGE

ROUND 15

1. Jess Hayes and Max Morley were the winners of which popular UK TV series?
2. Castelvetrano, Kalamata and Niçoise are all types of what?
3. +33 is the international dialling code for which country?
4. What does STEM stand for in education?
5. Which Miguel song returned to the *Billboard* Top 100 in 2022, after it first charted in 2011, thanks to TikTok?
6. Golden Touch, Paks and Shaba are all what?
7. According to the rules in Ludo, what happens if a player rolls a 6 three times?
8. What were the names of BBC's Chuckle Brothers?
9. What is the term for the office held by the pope?
10. To which YouTube collective do Aj Shabeel, KingKennyTV and Sharky belong?
11. 'Go', 'We're Not Kids Anymore' and 'Anxiety' are all songs by which artist?
12. Which law was repealed after the death of Stephen Lawrence in 2005?
13. Jerone Benjamin is the owner of which premium streetwear brand?
14. In 2021, which Black actor was named as the first female 007?
15. What does NBA stand for?

NOT-SO-GENERAL KNOWLEDGE

ROUND 16

1. During 2020, No Signal Radio started which competition between song choices?
2. Who was the voice of Frozone in the movie *The Incredibles*?
3. Which Nollywood actor represents the nightmare mother-in-law?
4. Name the August 2020 scheme created by Rishi Sunak whereby high-street restaurants were able to offer 50 per cent off on Mondays to Wednesdays that month to diners.
5. What was the Promised Land known as biblically?
6. Who played Stormtrooper Finn in *Star Wars: The Force Awakens* and *Star Wars: The Last Jedi*?
7. Where is the largest Waitrose in the UK located?
8. What does the ID in *i-D* magazine stand for?
9. Who founded the rap collective Flipmode Squad?
10. 'Heated', 'Cozy' and 'Church Girl' are all from which 2022 album?
11. Which actor plays the role of Bishop James Greenleaf?
12. Tolly Boy is a brand of what?
13. In *The Hunger Games*, what is the name for the special version of the games held every 25 years?
14. Young T & Bugsey's song went viral in 2020, a year after its release, sparking the name of which challenge during the Covid-19 lockdown?
15. Who released the song 'Santa Baby'?

NOT-SO-GENERAL KNOWLEDGE

ROUND 17

1. In what year were the following songs number 1 hits: 'Sound of the Underground', 'Dilemma', 'Round Round' and 'Crossroads'?
2. What does TED (from TED Talks) stand for?
3. What is nduja?
4. Which colour is traditionally associated with royalty and wealth?
5. Put the following in order from highest to lowest: alto, tenor, bass, soprano.
6. Miguel Rahiece Cunningham is the real name for which Birmingham-based UK rapper?
7. Malia and Sasha are the names of the daughters of which famous family?
8. 'My money don't _____ _____, it folds.' Fill in the blanks.
9. MD is the abbreviation for which US state?
10. What colour is the lid of Magnum, the popular tonic wine?
11. 'You are not in the UK, you are in Barbados' is a line from which TV show?
12. Finish the phrase 'Who has ever died from _____?'
13. Who wrote the book The Big O?
14. Who is the owner of Mavin records?
15. Who is regarded as the founding father of Manchester's Afro-Caribbean community?

NOT-SO-GENERAL KNOWLEDGE

ROUND 18

1. In 2022, streetwear brand Corteiz launched the 'Bolo Exchange'. What item of clothing were customers requested to bring?
2. What is Grace Jones's middle name?
3. In the card game blackjack, what does an 8 represent?
4. What is singer Adele's last name?
5. What does popular London sixth-form college SFX stand for?
6. The ram represents which sign of the zodiac?
7. Kéllé Bryan, Easther Bennett and Vernie Bennett were all part of which music group?
8. What alcohol is in the cocktail picante?
9. Name the three children featuring in the book written by Roderick Hunt that taught British children to read.
10. Who wrote the book *How Europe Underdeveloped Africa.*
11. Baroness Doreen Lawrence was given which recognition in 2003?
12. In a BBC series, Freema Agyeman rose to fame after starring as a companion to who?
13. Name the first female Black British newsreader to appear on BBC News.
14. Skepta's 'Nasty', Chip's 'Pepper Riddim' and Bugzy Malone 'Relegation Riddim' are examples of what?
15. Casyo 'Krept' Johnson and Sascha Ellese Gilbert are the owners of which brand?

NOT-SO-GENERAL KNOWLEDGE

ROUND 19

1. Vanessa Kingori became the first female publisher for which fashion magazine in 2017?
2. Olajide Olayinka Williams Olatunji is better known on the internet as what?
3. Gen Z officially begins in what year?
4. In the Bible, who had a multicoloured dream coat?
5. In 1984, Tessa Sanderson became the first Black woman to do what?
6. Juanita Bynum produces which genre of music?
7. Which prophet is mentioned most in the Qu'ran?
8. What did László Bíró invent?
9. Curve, Bold, Touch and Torch were all types of what?
10. Which image was the reason for the creation of Google images?
11. Which South African artist wrote the song 'Vuli Ndela'?
12. Chiwetel Ejiofor played the voice of which character in the 2019 remake of *The Lion King*?
13. According to the British proverb, what is the mother of invention?
14. Danish company Royal Unibrew are the owners of which popular drink, originally used as a dietary requirement to re-energise the troops?
15. In the Bible, what did Moses receive at the top of Mount Sinai?

NOT-SO-GENERAL KNOWLEDGE

ROUND 20

1. Muscat blanc grapes produce which type of wine?
2. How many players in total are on the court during a netball game?
3. 'Wash your hands, you detty pig' is a line said by which character in which series?
4. Celestial Church of Christ or Cherubim and Seraphim churches sit under which Christian denomination?
5. 'Hello, doctor' is heard in the intro to which UK-based podcast trio?
6. Who speaks as the voiceover in *Love Island*?
7. Put these consoles in order of their release: Game Boy Advance, Nintendo DS, Game Boy Color, GameCube, Nintendo 64.
8. What does the IC in IC3 stand for?
9. In what year was Jamal Edwards awarded his MBE?
10. What is the name of the album Little Simz released in 2021?
11. What size is a 'nip' or miniature alcohol bottle?
12. Which holiday is celebrated on 11 March in Cameroon?
13. Name the Afrobeat legend who married 27 women in 1978.
14. Scottish Fold, Ragamuffin and Chartreux are all types of what?
15. Dame Shirley Bassey lent her voice to three films from which movie franchise?

NOT-SO-GENERAL KNOWLEDGE

ROUND 21

1. The popular Ghanaian drink Alvaro is what kind of beverage?
2. How many days does Ramadan last for?
3. Kwanga is a staple in Congolese cuisine. What is it made of?
4. Who wrote the novel *The Color Purple*?
5. Bianca Saunders, ACW and Loudbrandstudios are all types of what?
6. Who was the first Black senator to be elected to the US Senate?
7. Name the popular Middle Eastern dish, originating in the Ottoman Empire, that consists of meat cut into thin slices, stacked in a cone-like shape and roasted on a slowly turning vertical rotisserie or spit.
8. Translate 'Inshallah'.
9. How is the BBC mainly funded?
10. Who was the first Black superhero to appear in a mainstream comic?
11. What geometric shape is generally used for stop signs?
12. Which vegetable is typically found in the West African dish efo riro?
13. What does AOB stand for in a meeting?
14. Amarula is a cream liqueur from which country?
15. As of January 2023, who is the MP for Hackney North and Stoke Newington?

NOT-SO-GENERAL KNOWLEDGE

ROUND 22

1. What is another term for 'flat iron' in relation to hair treatments?
2. How many Chinese signs of the zodiac are there?
3. A scone is typically referred to as what in the US?
4. What is the TV advert slogan for Tesco?
5. How many public holidays do the UK typically have a year?
6. Tequila, triple sec and lime juice make what cocktail?
7. What was the most popular boys name in the UK in 2022?
8. *I Know Why the Caged Bird Sings*, *Letter to My Daughter* and *Life Doesn't Frighten Me* are all books written by who?
9. What is the least spicy option you can get in Nando's?
10. In Christianity, name the partial fast in which meat, dairy, alcohol and other rich foods are avoided in favour of vegetables and water in order to be more sensitive to God.
11. The Ghanaian dish waakye is most popularly eaten at which mealtime of the day?
12. Muammar Gaddafi was the *de facto* leader of which country from 1969 to 2011?
13. What is the name of Cali Swag District's most successful track?
14. Tsebhi is one of the main traditional foods in Eritrea. What type of food is it?
15. Which three keys on a Mac do you need to hold together to take a screenshot?

NOT-SO-GENERAL KNOWLEDGE

ROUND 23

1. What does the UK slang term 'choong' mean?
2. Name the artist who made *Balloon Girl*.
3. Calamari is typically made with what ingredient?
4. Finish the sentence from the following viral TikTok sound, 'God Abeg, I don't want to be a mechanic . . .'
5. The Nigerian Civil War (1967–1970) was fought between Nigeria and who?
6. 'I am a logic-based, combinatorial number-placement puzzle.' What am I?
7. Kizomba, semba and bachata are all types of what?
8. In Judaism, a coming-of-age ritual for girls is referred to as what?
9. What phrase does TikTok content creator Benzo The1st typically use at the start of his videos?
10. In astrology, what are the three Earth signs?
11. Who wrote the book *Homegoing*?
12. What was the first video game console to receive universal acclaim?
13. What is the main ingredient in a falafel?
14. Name all members of WSTRN.
15. In Yoruba culture, who is the god of twins?

NOT-SO-GENERAL KNOWLEDGE

ROUND 24

1. What is Arsenal's Highbury Stadium now used for?
2. Who was the first Black openly gay actor to win an Emmy?
3. Arroz con maíz is a popular Latin American dish made with what two ingredients?
4. Name the *Black Mirror* episode which follows two old friends reconnecting over a virtual reality fighting game.
5. Growing up Black British in the 2000s, what was DAX used for?
6. Every Muslim is obligated to pray five times a day. What is the first prayer of the day called?
7. What is the traditional name for Ethiopian honey wine?
8. In 2022, Crocs collaborated with which Black-owned footwear designer on a new iteration of the famous clog?
9. According to the Myers–Briggs Type Indicator, how many personality types are there?
10. Korean skincare brand COSRX power essence gel has taken the skincare industry by storm. What is the main ingredient of the product?
11. How many jokers are there in a standard deck of cards?
12. Baptist, Methodist and Pentecostalism are all types of what?
13. Who makes up American hip hop duo City Girls?
14. 'I am a common baked British side dish, originally created by dipping batter in the fat around the roasted meat. I am most traditionally served alongside a Sunday roast.' What am I?
15. Kandi Burruss, Tameka 'Tiny' Cottle, LaTocha Scott, Tamera Coggins-Wynn and Tamika Scott formed which American girl group?

NOT-SO-GENERAL KNOWLEDGE

ROUND 25

1. Name the card game in which players deal cards and react quickly to spot pairs of cards of the same rank.
2. What year was streetwear brand Corteiz founded?
3. Catatos is a traditional Angolan dish. What is the main ingredient?
4. What ingredient is the peas in Jamaican rice and peas?
5. There are two main branches of Islam: Sunni and what?
6. Name the UK company owned by three brothers who offer the public a chance to win a new home for the price of a raffle ticket.
7. What is the fourth track on *The Miseducation of Lauryn Hill* album?
8. Who directed the music videos for Migos's 'Bad and Boujee', City Girls featuring Cardi B's 'Twerk' and Davido's 'Fall'?
9. Sky juice is a cocktail originating from which Caribbean island group?
10. Dawn Butler is the MP for which constituency?
11. Over half of Utah's population follow which religion?
12. As of February 2023, Viola Davis became the third Black woman in history to achieve EGOT status. Name the first two women.
13. 'NEPA take light' is a common phrase used in Nigeria when there is a power cut. What does NEPA actually stand for?
14. In the Bible, how many years did the children of Israel spend in the wilderness travelling to the Promised Land?
15. What is the machine often used in Pilates?

NOT-SO-GENERAL KNOWLEDGE

ROUND 26

1. What does BAE stand for?
2. Mobile network EE is a result of a merger of which two companies?
3. Which 'S' word in slang is used for someone who is slightly desperate, often doing too much for the person's attention they crave?
4. Diana Evans released a novel in 2018 that was shortlisted for the 2019 Women's Prize for Fiction. What is the novel called?
5. What does HIIT stand for?
6. Adam Nathaniel Williams is a British rapper better known as what?
7. The Gabi is a traditional dress worn in which African country?
8. What is the term used for Nigerian solid meals that are taken with soups and ingested by swallowing?
9. *The Long Song, Small Island* and *Fruit of the Lemon* are all novels written by which Black author?
10. Béarnaise or peppercorn sauce is often paired with what?
11. What month does Notting Hill Carnival take place?
12. What is the first word in the opening chapter of the Qur'an?
13. Matcha is finely ground powder of specially grown and processed what?
14. Name John Legend's wife.
15. What is 'We're Not Really Strangers'?

NOT-SO-GENERAL KNOWLEDGE

ROUND 27

1. Supermarket chain Morrisons bought and rebranded which supermarket?
2. Name all four members of the Black Eyed Peas at the height of their popularity in the 2000s.
3. What is the name of Mo Gilligan's 2022 Netflix special?
4. Alcohol brand Armand de Brignac is better known as what?
5. Chuck Taylor is which brand's classic shoe?
6. *The Kola Nut Does Not Speak English* is a theatre performance written and performed by which Black British Nigerian actor?
7. Vlookup is a function used on which computer programme?
8. Which country became the first in Europe to offer paid menstrual leave?
9. Father's Day is celebrated on the same day in both the UK and US. True or false?
10. What ingredient gives Rum Punch its red colour?
11. 'I Stay in Love', 'Bye Bye' and 'Touch My Body' are all tracks from which album? Both artist and album name needed.
12. What Christian denomination attends church on Saturdays?
13. Name the international private members' club that has venues in Shoreditch, Windsor, Brighton and Somerset.
14. Measurements of pHs less than 7 are classified as what?
15. Name the curl pattern one level looser than 4a.

NOT-SO-GENERAL KNOWLEDGE

ROUND 28

1. Guinness beer, vanilla Nutrament, sweetened condensed milk and vanilla typically make which cocktail?
2. Name Nigerian author Chinua Achebe's debut novel.
3. To 'lock' something means what in a UK slang context?
4. The Maasai people are a tribe originating from which region of Africa?
5. The competition whereby participants create teams from among the players in a league and score points according to the actual performance of their players is called what?
6. Name all five Dragons in the 2022 series of *Dragons' Den*.
7. What genre does DJ Black Coffee play?
8. Janet Daby has served as the MP for which constituency since 2018?
9. Which brand is behind the 'baby father baby shower' shirt?
10. Cassava is a root vegetable that can be poisonous unless you peel and cook it first. True or false?
11. What is AJ Odudu known for?
12. Who was the first winner of *American Idol*?
13. 'Just remember that you're the prize always' was advice shared between which celebrity father–daughter duo?
14. Beats Music and Beats Electronics were acquired by who in 2014?
15. An EU shoe size 39 is a UK size what?

NOT-SO-GENERAL KNOWLEDGE

ROUND 29

1. Tidal, Apple Music and Spotify are all types of what?
2. A haircut in the Black community is better referred to as what?
3. The singer and songwriter Donae'o makes what genre of music?
4. What is the official term for a legal assistant?
5. Roc Nation Brunch typically takes place just before which major music event?
6. 'Ebaba' or 'apa' is the word for 'father' in which language?
7. Caryn Elaine Johnson is professionally known as who?
8. In April 2022 Telfar announced a collaboration with which brand?
9. What colour is the compass on the distinctive Stone Island badge?
10. Name the religious ceremony for a Muslim couple to be legally wed under Islamic law.
11. Chuku's is a Nigerian restaurant based in north London specialising in a fusion with what style of food?
12. What is the spiciest wing flavour in Wingstop?
13. Clothing brands Daily Paper, Patta and Filling Pieces all hail from which European city?
14. What is Michelle Obama's bestselling 2018 memoir called?
15. Ghanaian chilli sauce is referred to as what?

NOT-SO-GENERAL KNOWLEDGE

ROUND 30

1. Rendition is a Black British platform that celebrates and connects audiences to what?
2. What US holiday is observed annually on the third Monday in January?
3. *Dawn*, *Kindred* and *Parable of the Sower* are all novels written by which author?
4. Where would you find an SPF rating?
5. How many times a year does London Fashion Week take place?
6. Which company acquired YouTube in 2006?
7. What character does actor Samira Wiley play in *The Handmaid's Tale*?
8. The 25 January Revolution refers to an uprising in which country?
9. 'Don't Let Me Fall', 'Sunshine' and 'Know That You Are Loved' are all songs on which British album? Both artist and album name needed.
10. What colour is the traditional fez hat?
11. Name the sweet South African snack with a sticky appearance that's prepared by frying braided dough strips in oil, then dunking them into a cold sugary syrup.
12. How many names is Allah said to have in Islam?
13. What is Marmite's brand slogan?
14. Name all three members of Mis-Teeq.
15. What does the acronym of online retailer ASOS stand for?

NOT-SO-GENERAL KNOWLEDGE

ROUND 31

1. What is SZA's debut album called?
2. Restaurant chain Blacklock is best known for what meal?
3. In Judaism, what is the compilation of the first five books of the Hebrew Bible called?
4. 'Summer in the Ends', 'Wicked' and 'Say You Love Me' are tracks off what album?
5. Which publishing house is Stormzy's Merky Books in partnership with?
6. Ursula Burns is known to be the first Black woman CEO of which type of company?
7. As of 2023, who is the world's richest woman?
8. 'The Lord's Prayer' is written in which book of the Bible?
9. Which term is the name for living a life of comfort and low stress?
10. Who is first non-classical or jazz artist to win the Pulitzer Prize for Music?
11. Name British author Bolu Babalola's debut anthology released in 2020.
12. Stork is a high-end central London based restaurant specialising in which cuisine?
13. In which venue did Beyoncé perform her London dates as part of her *Renaissance* world tour?
14. What is the main ingredient in traditional Moroccan tea?
15. Afrobeat artist Davido's preferred nickname is OBO. What does this stand for?

NOT-SO-GENERAL KNOWLEDGE

ROUND 32

1. What is the name of the covert government agency formerly in the popular political drama *Scandal*?
2. West African food staple fufu is typically made by using one of the three ingredients: cassava, yam and what?
3. What is the name of Kelechi Okafor's podcast?
4. Alcohol brand Kraken produces which spirit?
5. What is Tomi Obaro's debut novel titled?
6. In what part of an animal will you find the gizzard?
7. Sauvage, Black Opium and Daisy are all types of what?
8. 'Figures of Speech' was an exhibition shown at the Brooklyn Museum devoted to whose work?
9. Tigua dégué, which is rice with peanut sauce, is a traditional dish of which African country?
10. What is the unofficial US Black national anthem?
11. Which Hindu festival celebrates the eternal and divine love of the gods Radha and Krishna?
12. Name the second track on J Hus's *Common Sense* album.
13. *Closet Confessions* is a podcast starring TikTok stars Candice Brathwaite and who?
14. Which housewife iconically said 'Bye, Ashy'?
15. What year was *Avatar: The Way of Water* released?

NOT-SO-GENERAL KNOWLEDGE

ROUND 33

1. Where was the exhibition 'Soul of a Nation: Art in the Age of Black Power' showing in London back in 2017?
2. What is a chapati better known as in the Caribbean?
3. Who played Hoke Colburn in the film *Driving Miss Daisy*?
4. What is a Tasmiyah in Islam?
5. How many members form the Ezra Collective?
6. GCSE exams were formerly known as what?
7. What genre are the five albums that music collective SAULT released in 2022?
8. Name the US TV network that's home to the *Real Housewives* franchise.
9. Boukha is a Tunisian distilled beverage produced from which fruit?
10. British rapper Thyra Kigho Deshaun Oji is better known by what stage name?
11. Conna Walker is the CEO of which brand?
12. What is a courgette called in the US?
13. 'Love in the Dark' is a track off which Adele album?
14. Rhinoplasty is a surgical procedure that changes which part of the body?
15. Myrrh & Tonka is a bestselling scent from which brand?

NOT-SO-GENERAL KNOWLEDGE

ROUND 34

1. Which is the smallest continent?
2. Which X-Factor band were previously known as UFO before changing their name?
3. In the biblical story, who was put in the lion's den?
4. 'Toxic', 'Bad News' and 'Everybody Business' are tracks off which album? Both artist and album needed.
5. What does CSR in business stand for?
6. Sancocho is a traditional dish across Latin America. What type of food is it?
7. What is LOML an acronym for?
8. Niomi Arleen McLean-Daley is better known as who?
9. How many precepts are there in Buddhism?
10. Name Meagan Good's character in the TV series Harlem.
11. Oshikundu is a traditional drink made from cereal that is native to which African country?
12. Cult classic *Keisha the Sket* is written by who?
13. What is the name of Molly-Mae and Tommy Fury's child?
14. Precisely My Brow is a popular eyebrow pencil from what brand?
15. Jonah Hill and Lauren London star together in what Netflix film?

NOT-SO-GENERAL KNOWLEDGE

ROUND 35

1. In which book of the Bible can you find the longest chapter?
2. Beyoncé made history at the 2023 Grammys, having won the most lifetime Grammys ever. How many Grammys did she win to beat the previous record?
3. In miles, how far does the circulatory system in the human body stretch?
4. What word can be used to describe both a popular American dish and a mender of shoes?
5. *My Sister, the Serial Killer* is a novel written by who?
6. SLL is the currency code for which country?
7. The classic British chocolate bar Freddo remained at 10p until which year?
8. There are two major aircraft manufacturers in the commercial aviation sphere. One is Airbus. Name the second.
9. The very first iPhone was released in what year?
10. What is an anemometer used to measure?
11. 'You tough right?' is a quote taken from which cult classic movie?
12. In a standard deck of 52 cards, how many face cards are there?
13. Which artist created the score for HBO's *Euphoria*?
14. The closure of City Road station means that there's a large gap between Angel and Old Street. Which tube line is this on?
15. What was the bestselling game on Nintendo Wii?

NOT-SO-GENERAL KNOWLEDGE

ROUND 36

1. Viola Davis became part of the EGOT club in what year?
2. Who wrote the Songs of Songs in the Old Testament?
3. What is the currency code used in Belize?
4. UMD is a discontinued storage medium for the Sony PSP. What does UMD stand for?
5. What do you call a scientist who studies glaciers?
6. Who became the first Nigerian female artist to win a Grammy award?
7. What is the name of the colour that is opposite green on the colour wheel?
8. What is the maximum number of shots on a 35 mm roll of film?
9. Akala and Ms. Dynamite are siblings, true or false?
10. According to the *Guinness Book of World Records*, what is the world's hottest chilli pepper?
11. In British slang, what is SMH an abbreviation for?
12. Zamzam water is believed to be blessed holy water to which religious group?
13. 'From Bombay with Love' is the slogan of which popular UK restaurant chain?
14. Judi Love is widely recognised for her role as a panellist on *Loose Women*, but what was she originally known for?
15. What is the term used for people who do not believe in God?

NOT-SO-GENERAL KNOWLEDGE

ROUND 37

1. Most children in the UK start school full-time in the September following which birthday?
2. Coco Jones is an American singer and actor who rose to prominence after starring in which Disney Channel film?
3. What is the Indian film industry called?
4. How many people make up the R&B group Dvsn?
5. What is a chapter in the Qur'an called?
6. Black British designer Mary-Ann Msengi is behind which fashion label?
7. Which two Amapiano DJs are branded 'Scorpio Kings'?
8. Gin, Vermouth Rosso, Campari and an orange peel garnish typically make which cocktail?
9. American author Tayari Jones is best known for which novel?
10. In contemporary music, what does DnB stand for?
11. COS, ARKET, & Other Stories, Weekday and Monki are all under what group?
12. What is the official language of Gabon?
13. Who are Arabella's two best friends in the BBC drama series *I May Destroy You*?
14. Daniel Lena is the government name of which British rapper?
15. 'Situationship', 'Whoa' and 'Be Careful' are songs off which album? Artist and album name both needed.

NOT-SO-GENERAL KNOWLEDGE

ROUND 38

1. What is the main ingredient in the Puerto Rican dish mofongo?
2. The legendary 2004 gladiator Pepsi advert starred which four singers?
3. Soukous is a genre of dance music found in which African countries?
4. In which book of the Bible can you find the shortest chapter?
5. What is the geographical reference line that passes through the Royal Observatory in Greenwich called?
6. What is said to be the national drink of Kenya?
7. Name the government department responsible for inspecting a range of educational institutions, including state schools and some independent schools, in England.
8. 'Necking' is a term used in northern England. What does it mean?
9. Who is the first Black woman to win Record of the Year at the Grammys this century?
10. Finish the following popular TikTok sound: 'If it's the same stuff I ate last night, forget it . . .'
11. What is rapper Little Simz's first name?
12. What date is considered to be an unlucky day in Western superstition?
13. Puff puff, the popular Nigerian snack, is referred to as what in Malawi?
14. How many children does British YouTuber Patricia Bright have?
15. What is the first track on Headie One's *Edna* album?

NOT-SO-GENERAL KNOWLEDGE

1. What does it mean to be teetotal?
2. Which artist is behind the following songs: 'Second Sermon', 'Kwaku the Traveller' and 'Soja'.
3. What year did the first ever MOBO Awards take place?
4. What does NSFW stand for?
5. What are Walkers crisps called across Europe?
6. What is the term for the process of urban development in which a city neighbourhood develops rapidly over a short time, changing from low to high value.
7. Which two ingredients typically accompany eggs in a Nigerian breakfast?
8. Brenda Wireko Mensah is professionally known as who?
9. Which 'M' describes those reportedly able to mediate between familiar spirits or the spirits of the dead and living human beings?
10. What is the classic Senegalese robe called?
11. The Decalogue is commonly known as what?
12. 'Pick Up Your Feelings', 'On It' and 'Lost One' are songs on which album? Both artist and album name are needed.
13. Amasi is a popular beverage in South Africa that is made from which product?
14. In colloquial terms, what does IYKYK stand for?
15. Who was famously branded 'America's Most Hated Housewife' after her first season on *The Real Housewives of Beverly Hills*?

NOT-SO-GENERAL KNOWLEDGE

ROUND 40

1. Which Spanish dance when translated to English means 'double step'?
2. What month has the shortest day of the year in the UK?
3. Who wrote the self-help book *What a Time to Be Alone*?
4. For how many days was Kwasi Kwarteng the chancellor of the exchequer under Liz Truss's government?
5. What sexual orientation is defined as experiencing no sexual feelings, attraction or desires to anyone?
6. At which occasion did Jesus turn water into wine?
7. What is the advanced exercise programme that involves bodyweight exercises and high-intensity interval training? Workouts are usually performed 20 to 60 minutes at a time, 6 days a week for 60 days.
8. Kwaito is a music genre that emerged from which country?
9. NARS, Too Faced and Morphe are all what?
10. Which year was the teenage classic *Bring It On: All or Nothing* released?
11. A djellaba is a long, full-sleeved, loose-fitting unisex robe worn in which region of Africa?
12. What is the final song on Rihanna's *ANTI* album?
13. What nationality is beauty influencer Jackie Aina's partner?
14. Kitcha is a flatbread from which East African country?
15. What do Americans usually call solicitors?

NOT-SO-GENERAL KNOWLEDGE

ROUND 41

1. Why is The Dunes apartment complex in LA famous?
2. What is the national dish of Zimbabwe?
3. Who created and performed the 2018 play *Misty*?
4. What is the term for a professional labour assistant who provides physical and emotional support to families during pregnancy, childbirth and the postpartum period?
5. How many letters are there in the Arabic alphabet?
6. TV host Trevor Noah is a staple on American television but which country is he originally from?
7. How much was Rihanna paid for her 2023 Super Bowl halftime performance?
8. Jedidiah Duyile is the owner of which brand famously worn by the likes of Kylie Jenner and Tems?
9. Which *Love Island* custom usually takes place halfway through the show and is often described as the 'ultimate test' of the islanders' relationships?
10. Who was the first Black woman to win five Grammy awards in one night?
11. What is the primary alcohol typically used in a bramble cocktail?
12. Who wrote the novel *Their Eyes Were Watching God*?
13. What is the keyboard shortcut to hide a selected row on Excel?
14. 'Karma', relating to the principle of cause and effect, is a word from which language?
15. Name the process when discarded objects or materials are reused to create a product of higher quality or value than the original.

NOT-SO-GENERAL KNOWLEDGE

ROUND 42

1. When three flashing red lights appear on your Xbox 360, what is it called?
2. How many feet are in a yard?
3. Which professional footballer used the alias Baby Jet to release music?
4. What is the name of the large egg-shaped super fruit with dried and hardened pulp inside?
5. In the Bible, what is the shortest letter St Paul wrote?
6. In 2022's 'The World's 50 Best Bars' list, which city was home to the most bars?
7. In 2008 Kobe Bryant appeared in a Nike commercial jumping over what car model?
8. In forex, what is the unit of measurement to express the change in value between two currencies?
9. Which type of compass uses the Earth's magnetic field?
10. What is the title of British *Vogue* editor-in-chief Edward Enninful's autobiography?
11. Rum, Curaçao, orgeat syrup and lime juice make up which cocktail?
12. In February 2023 football pundit Micah Richards revealed he pays how much per haircut?
13. Only 24 out of 54 countries had CAF-approved stadiums for the qualifiers of which 2023 tournament?
14. In Greek mythology, what is Morpheus the god of?
15. Which sovereign city state within Europe has banned the use of Uber?

NOT-SO-GENERAL KNOWLEDGE

ROUND 43

1. Who played Vincent Hubbard in *EastEnders* from 2015 to 2018?
2. E3 is an annual trade event for the video game industry in the US. What is E3 short for?
3. World Chase Tag® is the global league for competitive tag. What year was it founded?
4. It was announced in 2023 that after 50 years soft drink Lilt will be rebranded to what drink?
5. *The Native*, *Gal-dem* and *New Wave* are all examples of Black-owned what?
6. What is the 'Raya' app mostly used for?
7. Which celebrity said the following: 'I definitely want Brooklyn to be christened, but I don't know into what religion yet'?
8. What is the capital of Mali?
9. Which profession is the PGCE course for?
10. 'Voices', 'Purple Heart' and 'Screwface Capital' are tracks off which album? Both artist and album name are needed.
11. Where is said to be the first holy site of Christianity?
12. What is the debut 2018 collaborative album by the Carters called?
13. British national African-Caribbean newspaper *The Voice* was founded in what year?
14. Who was announced as Louis Vuitton's next men's creative director in February 2023?
15. Jasmine Braithwaite and Victoria Sanusi are co-hosts of which British podcast?

NOT-SO-GENERAL KNOWLEDGE

ROUND 44

1. What is the chemical symbol for silver?
2. According to the Book of Genesis in the Bible, what did God do on the fourth day of creation?
3. Why was Earn arrested in the first season of the TV series *Atlanta*?
4. Put Google, Amazon and Netflix in order of age from youngest to oldest.
5. In the *Harry Potter* books, what is the rare wizardly ability that Harry and Voldemort share?
6. Barack Obama first won office back in 2008. He was elected over which Republican?
7. What is the name of the procession that takes place on Sunday morning at Notting Hill Carnival?
8. What is the name of the exam that London black cab drivers are required to complete?
9. Which fruit would you most typically find accompanying a Somali dish?
10. What are birds of the same feather said to do?
11. Independent record label YBNL formed by Afrobeat artist Olamide is home to artists such as Asake and Fireboy DML. What does YBNL stand for?
12. Westminster Council announced in November 2022 that they will no longer use the term 'BAME'. Which term are they replacing it with?

13. Name all four French Caribbean islands.
14. What girl's name is also used to refer to Christmas songs?
15. How many members make up the popular British podcast *Pass the Meerkat*?

NOT-SO-GENERAL KNOWLEDGE

ROUND 45

1. Which artist sang on 'Big Rich Town', the original theme song for the TV series *Power*?
2. Which of Santa's reindeer shares the same name as the 'God of love' of Valentine's Day?
3. Agbo jedi-jedi is a herbal remedy used to treat which part of the body?
4. Name the highball cocktail typically made with dark rum and ginger beer served over ice and garnished with a slice of lime.
5. Birds of Paradise, Queen's Tears and Weeping Fig are all types of what?
6. Lord Shorty is said to be the 'father' of which music genre?
7. How many points is the letter 'B' worth on a *Scrabble* board?
8. Which of the following names were *not* said in the chorus of the Wizkid classic 'Pakurumo'? Folake, Fisayo, Halima, Tolani.
9. What 'X' is the fear of foreigners or strangers?
10. What is often considered to be the national dish of Algeria, Morocco and Tunisia?
11. If you were born on 25 April, what star sign are you?
12. In May 2022, the BBC announced that they will be closing which two channels by 2025?
13. In the Caribbean, which plant is known as a 'sinkle bible'?
14. What word is found between Alpha and Charlie in the NATO phonetic alphabet?
15. Name the primarily Muslim ethnic group that exist across Africa, whose name doubles as a style of braids.

NOT-SO-GENERAL KNOWLEDGE

ROUND 46

1. The dance known as 'the candy' is called what in the US?
2. What does a Craig David cocktail consist of?
3. Which sign of the zodiac is represented by the crab?
4. Yung Filly went out three nights in a row and had a bill for the DJ if they could play which song, by which artist? Both song title and artist are needed.
5. What does AAVE stand for?
6. 'In a Minute' by Lil Baby and 'Pound Cake' by Drake feature the same sample from which artist?
7. Who is the Roman goddess of love?
8. Branded as one of the Caribbean's largest parties, name the three-day event that took place in Negril in July/August 2022.
9. Wholegrain, Dijon and English are varieties of which condiment?
10. What is the key ingredient in the Nigerian street food suya that gives it its unique flavour?
11. Which radio station did a divorcee call into at the beginning of 'Kiss Kiss' by Chris Brown?
12. During Ramadan, what do Muslims traditionally drink at breakfast?
13. *Barbershop 2*, *Nope* and *Hustlers* all have which actor in common?
14. If you dialled +1 at the beginning of an international call, would you be calling the US or Australia?
15. Which of the following MCs/rappers is *not* from east London: Tempa T, Wretch 32, Kano?

NOT-SO-GENERAL KNOWLEDGE

ROUND 47

1. What is the British name for the fresh herb that's called cilantro in the US?

2. *Cut Both Ways, Sista Sister* and *I Am Not Your Baby Mother* are books written by which author?

3. In September 2022, which brand announced they were giving away their company in a bid to fight climate change?

4. On HBO's latest hit show *House of the Dragon,* who is known as the Sea Snake?

5. Name the highly selective East Ham sixth-form college that boasts 90 per cent of its students achieving A*s/A's in 2022 and gaining 85 Oxbridge offers.

6. Which of these albums was *not* released in 2021: *Pretty Bitch Music* by Saweetie, *Shiesty Season* by Pooh Shiesty, *Send Them to Coventry* by Pa Salieu?

7. Which video game was discontinued on PlayStation and Xbox in July 2021?

8. The poem 'Still I Rise' was written by who?

9. Name one of just two African countries which have never been colonised by Europeans.

10. Music network Channel AKA was formerly known as what?

11. What fruit juice is in a piña colada?

12. 'The future belongs to those who prepare for it today' is a quote by which civil rights leader?

13. What was the name of the annual street festival that took place in Brixton from 2006 to 2016?

14. Which singer had a 2012 hit with 'Diamonds'?

15. Which month is Black History Month in the US?

NOT-SO-GENERAL KNOWLEDGE

ROUND 48

1. What does EGOT stand for?
2. In October 2022 Vybz Kartel made news for doing what from his jail cell?
3. In Season 3 of *Real Housewives of Atlanta*, how much was Gregg Leakes accused of borrowing from Dwight Eubanks?
4. What does HBCUs stand for?
5. What did my true love give to me on the ninth day of Christmas?
6. What is the main ingredient found in Nigerian dish moi moi?
7. What club are you said to join if you have sexual intercourse on a plane?
8. In the Netflix original American anime series *Neo Yokio*, what is the first name of the person that Kaz got as a Secret Santa?
9. In the show *Rick and Morty*, what did Rick turn himself into to avoid going to family therapy?
10. In which city was Mohammed (PBUH) born?
11. What is the main ingredient in rum?
12. In the first *Home Alone* film, what city were Kevin's family going on holiday to?
13. In Judaism, a coming-of-age ritual for boys is referred to as what?
14. Name all four *Girlfriends* characters (first names are fine). A point for each name.
15. Who is the actor voicing the character of the adult Simba in the 2019 remake of *The Lion King*?

NOT-SO-GENERAL KNOWLEDGE

ROUND 49

1. Who was the president of the United States in 2005?
2. In Season 5 of *Love Island*, Ovie Soko shouted 'Message!' every time someone received a text on the show. Which film was he referencing?
3. What are the first three words in the Bible?
4. Vodka, peach schnapps, orange juice and cranberry juice typically make what cocktail?
5. Who came up with the phrase 'Jinky mi Jinky'?
6. According to Fredo, what dish can we not feed the badders?
7. Which chess piece can only move diagonally?
8. Which two rappers released the song 'Finally Rich' in 2015?
9. Which spirit is most commonly used when making an old fashioned?
10. In July 2021 Matt Hancock was caught in 4K, cheating with his aide. What is her name?
11. What is the Arabic word for the Friday prayer practised by Muslims?
12. Which beauty influencer owns the lifestyle brand named FORVR Mood?
13. Cilest, Microgynon and Rigevidon are all types of what?
14. Who plays the character Molly Carter in *Insecure*?
15. What is prepared in a tannery?

NOT-SO-GENERAL KNOWLEDGE

ROUND 50

1. K Koke, Nines and Riz Ahmed all hail from which London borough?
2. Name two of the three angels who are mentioned in the Protestant Bible.
3. Name the web-based game whose success led to its acquisition by *The New York Times*.
4. Idi Amin was the former leader of which country?
5. More food is eaten in the US on Thanksgiving than on any other day. Which day comes second?
6. In *Attack on Titan*, what was the name of the royal family before they constructed the three walls?
7. Biltong is a form of dry cured meat popular in which part of Africa?
8. On the popular London podcast *90s Baby Show*, if you make a mistake or say something stupid, this is known as a _____ offence?
9. What word is used to describe a short, traditional saying, stating a general truth or piece of advice?
10. Who wrote the book *Nearly All the Men in Lagos Are Mad*?
11. On the Netflix reality TV show *Young, Famous & African*, what phrase do some cast members often use to refer to champagne?
12. In Ghanaian culture, what is the name given to a female child born on a Saturday?
13. What is the main ingredient in Japanese saké?
14. In a tin of Quality Street, what colour wrapper is the fudge chocolate piece?
15. What does EMEA stand for?

NOT-SO-GENERAL KNOWLEDGE

ROUND 51

1. Julie, Ify, Joseph and Jamie are first names from which legendary Black British family?
2. What is the name of the best hand in poker?
3. In the Bible, who was turned into a pillar of salt?
4. Which podcast is hosted by 6ft+ of pure temptation & the coldest co-host in co-host history?
5. RMD are the initials for which famous Nollywood actor?
6. What chemical compound is known as 'laughing gas'?
7. Since the first release in 2008, how many Marvel Cinematic Universe movies have there been as of March 2023?
8. In 2006 T-Mobile launched a deal for Pay As You Go customers. For a small fee, customers were given unlimited usage for a set number of days. What was the name of the deal?
9. What is the Arabic name of the procedure Muslims carry out before prayer?
10. In *Game of Thrones*, during the battle against the Army of the Dead, which brave soul sacrificed their life while killing a giant?
11. Name a US state beginning with the letter K.
12. In Western astrology, zodiac signs are said to relate to the four elements. Gemini, Libra and Aquarius relate to which of the elements?
13. In the 2011 version of *Hunter × Hunter*, how many members are there in the phantom troupe?

14. 'You Can't Save Me', 'Still Blue' and 'The Recipe' are tracks on which album? One point for the correct artist name, one point for the correct album name.
15. Ra'Nell was one of the main characters in crime drama *Top Boy*. What was the name of his best friend?

NOT-SO-GENERAL KNOWLEDGE

ROUND 52

1. Justin, Chance, Quincy and Jessie James are just some of the names of the children born to which rap legend?
2. What is the term given to media photographers who follow or even hound well-known public figures?
3. Which Black British-born make-up artist's beauty brand is valued at $1 billion?
4. What is the name of Munya Chawawa's news reading alter ego?
5. What 'L' is the name given to a Nobel Prize winner?
6. What's the name of a form of freestyle in music, as well as the West Indian term for 'malevolent spirit' or 'ghost'?
7. Which popular spirit is distilled from the agave cactus?
8. What animal is used as an acronym for a person who is the best in their respective field?
9. Which smoked fish might you expect to be served with cream cheese and lemon juice in canapes?
10. Up, Down, Left, Right, Left, Right, Left, Right are instructions for which dance?
11. Name the song by the following artists: Kanye West, Jay-Z, Rick Ross, Nicky Minaj and Bon Iver.
12. What do the stars represent on the flag of the US?
13. Beyoncé, Adele and Lionel Richie have all released a song called what?
14. In the UK, the longest day of the year occurs in which month?
15. What was Diane Abbott spotted drinking on the tube back in 2019?

NOT-SO-GENERAL KNOWLEDGE

ROUND 53

1. Which luxury-car headquarters are Santan Dave and Stormzy in during the music video for *Clash*?
2. Who was president of Nigeria from May 1999 to May 2007?
3. What is the name given to describe the oldest and most prestigious universities in the US?
4. Psalms, Romans, Exodus and Proverbs: which of these books are *not* in the Old Testament of the Bible?
5. What shape are stop signs in the UK?
6. What name was given to the 2016 scandal involving 1.5 million leaked documents exposing the dark secrets of the financial industry?
7. In Jamaican patois, what does the word 'mauger' mean?
8. What is the name of the location that was struck by a meteor in Season 4 of *Fortnite*?
9. Ntaba is a dish originating from which countries?
10. Ogbono, the popular West African dish, is made from the seeds of which fruit?
11. Name the elephant-headed Hindu god of beginnings.
12. Which brand was originally called Blue Ribbon Sports?
13. 'London Landlord' Giggs pleaded with the 'youths of today' in a tweet, asking them to try and have only one what?
14. How many months pregnant was the female protagonist in Usher's song 'Confessions Part II'?
15. Which diss track specialist has released songs called 'Pepper Riddim', 'Coward' and 'Duppy'?

NOT-SO-GENERAL KNOWLEDGE

ROUND 54

1. The songs 'Trust Issues', 'Tinder' and 'Why Stress' are from which studio album? Both artist and album name are needed.
2. In Greek mythology, Hera is the goddess of what?
3. Put the following in order of height (tallest to shortest): Yaya Touré, Usain Bolt and Stormzy.
4. Cuba, Barbados, Luxembourg and Zimbabwe all have a legal drinking age of what?
5. In Judaism, what is the day of rest called which takes place on Friday evening to Saturday evening?
6. Waragi is an alcoholic beverage from which country?
7. In the anime series *Naruto*, Killer B is the jinchūriki of which tailed beast?
8. Name the four train stations on a Monopoly set.
9. Name the popular Louisiana dish that consists of a strongly flavoured stock, meat or shellfish, a thickener, celery, bell peppers and onions.
10. Which luxury clothing brand is also the name for the Greek god of commerce, eloquence and invention?
11. In Cockney rhyming slang, if you are 'cut and carried' you are what?
12. Name the non-alcoholic drink that is traditionally made up of a mix of Fanta, Sprite, cucumber, lemon, grenadine and Angostura bitters.
13. In astrology, what are the three water signs?
14. Native to the Caribbean, what sort of animal is the mountain chicken?
15. What was the name of Drake's first number 1 single in the UK?

NOT-SO-GENERAL KNOWLEDGE

ROUND 55

1. In which London borough can you find the barber shop D&Ls?

2. Which of the following one-hit-wonders had the highest net worth: Lou Bega ('Mambo No. 5'), Afroman ('Because I Got High') or Vanilla Ice ('Ice Ice Baby')?

3. Where in the human body would you find the medulla oblongata?

4. Vodka, ginger beer and lime juice make what cocktail?

5. Name the band consisting of members J-Rock, Nadia, Cherise and Randy who had hits with 'OK' and 'Favourite Things'.

6. What part of London is referred to as 'Little Lagos'?

7. Name the men's HBCU that has a close affiliation to Spelman College.

8. Plan B released a track in 2007 based around telling his friend about his predicament of falling in love with a girl much younger than himself. What was the title of this song?

9. Name all seven artists on Young Money's track 'BedRock'.

10. At which London station is platform 9¾ located?

11. Day26, O-Town and Danity Kane were all formed on which show?

12. Name the longest-running collective album for UK classics, which began in 1982.

13. *NW, Swing Time* and *White Teeth* are novels written by which author?
14. Who became the first UK rapper to reach over 1 billion streams on Spotify Wrapped?
15. Name the 'Home Run' singer who came forth in 2011's The X Factor.

NOT-SO-GENERAL KNOWLEDGE

ROUND 56

1. How do you say 'Season's Greetings' in Yoruba? E kun ___?
2. Lori Harvey gave a viral red-carpet interview back in May 2022 revealing her toned physique was a result of what?
3. Name the 2022 storm that removed parts of the roof at the O2 Arena.
4. In October 2022 Rihanna debuted 'Lift Me Up', her first solo single in how many years?
5. How old was Queen Elizabeth II at the time of her passing?
6. How many weeks was Liz Truss prime minister for?
7. COLC is an acronym for what?
8. What did Stormy Wellington go viral for describing her friend's food as?
9. Knucks, M Huncho, Miraa May and Little Simz all shared category nominations for which award at the 2022 MOBOs?
10. In Cardi B's verse on the 'Thotiana' remix, what two things does the rapper say she will leave his breath smelling like?
11. The 'About Love' campaign and film featuring Jay-Z and Beyoncé was created for their partnership with which brand?
12. Damini Ebunoluwa Ogulu is the government name for which artist?
13. *All About Love* is a book written by which Black author?
14. Who is the half-blood prince in *Harry Potter*?
15. GUAP were appointed creative agency for which luxury brand in 2021?

2

ARE YOU SMARTER THAN A 10-YEAR-OLD?

In this round we are taking you back to school, so these questions should all be simple . . . Right? The answers can be found on pages 255–260.

ARE YOU SMARTER THAN A 10-YEAR-OLD?

ROUND 1

1. What is the name of the pigment in plants that makes them turn green?
2. Frogs belong to which animal group?
3. Name the patchwork elephant from the popular childhood books.
4. Political parties publish a declaration outlining promises and plans if they are elected. What is this declaration called?
5. Translate the following from German to English: *Ich liebe dich.*
6. How many teeth should an adult have including their wisdom teeth?
7. In *The Lion King*, what kind of animal is Pumbaa?
8. Edexcel, AQA and OCR are all what?
9. Kenza is 54 years old and her mother is 80. How many years ago was Kenza's mother three times Kenza's age?
10. True or false – the earth's moon gives off its own light?
11. Which utensil do you use to draw a circle?
12. What is the word for the colour yellow in Spanish?
13. What is (38 − 66) + 50, with the answer expressed in Roman numerals?
14. The prime minister chooses ministers for important government departments. What do these ministers form?
15. Jade drove from Birmingham to London for Garage Nation. Given that her average speed was 50 mph, how many hours and minutes did it take her to travel 120 miles?

ARE YOU SMARTER THAN A 10-YEAR-OLD?

ROUND 2

1. Name the nationalities of the following countries: Denmark, Malta, Somalia.
2. What is the date of the first day of the 20th century?
3. What is a species without a backbone known as?
4. *James and the Giant Peach*, *The Witches* and *The Twits* are books all written by who?
5. What is the name for materials that will not carry any electric charge?
6. What four countries make up the UK?
7. What is the chemical symbol for iron?
8. Thinking back to ICT, how do you create a hyperlink for highlighted text using Microsoft shortcuts?
9. During the 2000s Tádé had Usher stickers on her wall. The space she had available was 55 cm by 60 cm and the stickers were each 15 cm by 5 cm. What was the maximum number of stickers Tádé could fit on the wall?
10. What is the word for words that sound the same but have different meanings?
11. Palaeontology is the study of what?
12. Translate the following from Spanish to English: *'¿Cómo te llamas?'*
13. What is the more common name for the patella?
14. If a hen and a half lays an egg and a half in a day and a half, how many eggs will half a dozen hens lay in half a dozen days?
15. What is the name for an animal that eats both plants and meat?

ARE YOU SMARTER THAN A 10-YEAR-OLD?

ROUND 3

1. How many people sit on a jury of a criminal trial in the UK?
2. What is the name for a female fox?
3. Grandad Yusef left half his money to his granddaughter and half that amount to his grandson. He left a sixth to his brother, and the remainder, £1,000, to a local charity. How much did he leave altogether?
4. How many elements are there in the Periodic Table?
5. Fill in the blanks from this assembly classic: 'I was cold, I was naked, were you there? And the _____ and the _____, and the _____ won't matter, were you there?'
6. There are 25 packs of Indomie in a box. A shop orders 14 boxes. How many packs did the shop order?
7. Which planet is the third from the sun?
8. What is the plural of ox?
9. A tetradecagon has how many sides?
10. What is the unit of measurement for pulse rate?
11. In mathematics, what is 6 factorial?
12. How many years are there in a millennium?
13. If Kunle is facing west and turns 180 degrees to his right, what direction is he facing now?
14. If you count from 1 to 100, how many 7s will you pass on the way?
15. What is the pH of pure water at room temperature?

ARE YOU SMARTER THAN A 10-YEAR-OLD?

ROUND 4

1. What does R&B stand for?
2. What are the parts of the globe located above or below the equator called?
3. What do we call a group of geese on the ground?
4. Ayomide likes 25 not 24, 400 but not 300, 121 not 122. Does he like 1,600 or 2,000?
5. Which word represents 'Q' in the NATO phonetic alphabet?
6. How do you write the number 214 in Roman numerals?
7. Zainab had 15 boxes of 40 pencils. She lost 15 pencils. How many pencils does she have now?
8. Spell 'ibuprofen'.
9. If you flip a coin 10 times, how many times are you guaranteed it will land on heads?
10. What are the three states of matter?
11. What is the *full* name of the main character in the young adult book *Holes*?
12. A market sells 40 boxes of plantain. A box contains trays of plantain. There are 15 plantains in a tray. There are 3 trays in a box. How many plantains does the supermarket sell?
13. Who wrote the novel *Oliver Twist*?
14. What two systems help us get nutrients from our food and deliver them throughout our body?
15. How many time zones are there on earth?

ARE YOU SMARTER THAN A 10-YEAR-OLD?

ROUND 5

1. Who wrote the poem 'Half-caste'?
2. There were some people at a dancery. 19 people leave at midnight. 17 people arrive at 1am. Now there are 63 people at the dancery. How many people were in the dance to begin with?
3. What is the largest animal in the world?
4. How often are general elections held in the UK?
5. Name the first five prime numbers.
6. What does PEE stand for in English?
7. Translate the following sentence to French: 'I live in London.'
8. How many wheels do 99 bicycles and one tricycle have?
9. I am an odd number. Take away one letter and I become even. What number am I?
10. Correctly finish the sentence of to this song: 'Give me oil in my lamp keep me burning, give me oil in my lamp I pray, give me oil in my lamp keep me burning, Keep me burning til' . . .'
11. Spell 'mannequin'.
12. Isosceles is one category of triangle measured by side length. Name the other two.
13. Which of the seven continents is the least populated?
14. There is a three-digit number. The second digit is four times as big as the third digit, while the first digit is three less than the second digit. What is the number?
15. The _____ of a number is another number that produces the first number when it is multiplied by itself?

ARE YOU SMARTER THAN A 10-YEAR-OLD?

ROUND 6

1. Spell the word 'nauseous'.
2. In science, how would you describe a material that can be dissolved in a liquid?
3. *El caballo* is what animal in Spanish?
4. A bag of marbles contains six purple marbles and two white marbles. A marble is taken from the bag. What is the probability it is white?
5. Local governments are commonly known as what?
6. What unit of measurement is used to measure sound intensity?
7. What is the name of the lion in *The Lion, the Witch and the Wardrobe*?
8. If the cost of a Maggi cube and an onion combined is £1.10 and the onion costs £1.00 more than the Maggi cube, how much does the Maggi cost?
9. Your hypothalamus is found in which part of the body?
10. Abiola has the same number of brothers as she has sisters. Each one of her brothers has 50 per cent more sisters than brothers. How many children are in Abiola's family?
11. What were the names of Harry Potter's parents?
12. Spell 'Albuquerque'.
13. How many zeros are in 1 billion?
14. The process of dividing a cell and its nucleus into two cells that each have their own nucleus is known as what?
15. At the end of the Middle Ages there was a rebirth of classical philosophy, literature, culture and art. What is this period known as?

ARE YOU SMARTER THAN A 10-YEAR-OLD?

ROUND 7

1. There are four numbers. If we leave out any one number, the average of the remaining three numbers will be 45, 60, 65 or 70. What is the average of all four numbers?
2. What term is used to describe the process when water vapour becomes liquid?
3. Sarah uses a discount code to purchase her Pretty Little Thing order. Her basket total falls from £1,000 to £650 after applying a discount code. What was the percentage of her discount?
4. In the novel *Of Mice and Men*, what is the name of the character who gets killed at the hands of Lennie at the end of the film?
5. Born in 1729, Ignatius Sancho was the first Black Briton to do what?
6. Which is the second-largest country in Africa by square miles?
7. Femi, who is 20 years old, is four times as old as Mary. How old will he be when he's twice as old as her?
8. The ' denominator' refers to the bottom half of a fraction. What is the top half called?
9. What is the plural of moose?
10. Olajuwon has to make popcorn for himself and five siblings. With each sibling eating two and half packs, how many packs must Olajuwon make?
11. What is the largest number that can be pronounced as a single syllable?

12. Spell 'conscientious'.
13. How many hydrogen atoms are in one molecule of water?
14. What are the comparative and superlative forms of the word 'big?'
15. A bucket holds 5 litres of water. 250 ml of water is drained from the bucket every minute. How many minutes will it take for the bucket to be empty?

ARE YOU SMARTER THAN A 10-YEAR-OLD?

ROUND 8

1. Name the title of the second book in Malorie Blackman's *Noughts & Crosses* series.
2. Huron, Ontario, Michigan, Erie and Superior are the names of what?
3. Who wrote the novel *To Kill a Mockingbird*?
4. Abdul gets to a train station at 3.54pm, 15 minutes early for his train to Lewisham and his train arrives 8 minutes late. What time does his train depart?
5. Haematology is the branch of medicine involving the study of what?
6. If Phyllis is facing north-west and turns 90 degrees to her left, in which direction is she facing now?
7. If 1 August falls on a Tuesday, what day will it be on the final day of the month?
8. We all remember taking PSHE lessons here and there during school but what does PSHE actually stand for?
9. If Precious divides 111,111 by 11, what number does she get?
10. What does the French word '*meubles*' mean?
11. Which quadrilateral has one pair of parallel sides with different lengths?
12. What is the superlative of many?
13. The bassoon is a member of which musical family?
14. Which weighs more, 10 stone or 60 kg?
15. What is the process by which green plants and some other organisms use sunlight to derive nutrients from carbon dioxide and water?

ARE YOU SMARTER THAN A 10-YEAR-OLD?

ROUND 9

1. Bola is three years younger than Mohammed. Mohammed is seven years older than Andrew. How much older than Andrew is Bola?
2. What is the name for an animal that eats only plants?
3. What is the title of the last book in the *Harry Potter* series?
4. How many planets are there in our solar system?
5. What are the three primary colours?
6. What is the name for a male chicken?
7. How many sides does a nonagon have?
8. What are the two prime numbers that add up to 13?
9. What is the chemical symbol for lead?
10. What is the largest newspaper format called?
11. A person who believes that nothing is known or can be known of the existence of God is called what?
12. True or false? A triangle can have two acute angles.
13. Name both houses in the British Parliament.
14. On what date is International Women's Day celebrated every year?
15. What is the flag of the UK known as?

ARE YOU SMARTER THAN A 10-YEAR-OLD?

ROUND 10

1. Spell 'fuchsia'.
2. What is 1,202 + 45 + 367?
3. What is Benjamin Zephaniah most famous for?
4. How many square numbers are there between 101 and 200?
5. What colour do red and blue make?
6. What is the chemical symbol for neon?
7. How many minutes are in 8 hours?
8. What is the name for a female horse?
9. Members of which political party traditionally wear red rosettes at elections?
10. Which planet is closest to the sun?
11. What number is also known as a 'dozen'?
12. What does MP stand for?
13. What is the name of the tooth that is used to grip and tear food?
14. What type of animal is a turtle?
15. What is the name of the green Teletubby?

3

A QUESTION OF SPORT

From football and basketball to athletics and dance, this round does what it says on the tin: we're talking all things sport. The answers can be found on pages 260–270.

A QUESTION OF SPORT

ROUND 1

1. During the 2017/18 Premier League season, who was the only team to win the majority of their points away from home?

2. Which player beat Serena Williams in the 2018 US Open final?

3. In which sport would you find the move 'a Full Nelson'?

4. As of 2022, how many times has Anthony Joshua been a unified heavyweight world champion?

5. Name the two athletes who beat Usain Bolt in the final of the 2017 World Athletics Championships 100 metres.

6. According to *Forbes*, who is the world's highest-paid athlete as of 2022?

7. In 2018 Luka Modrić won the Ballon d'Or. Name the woman that won the Ballon d'Or Féminin that year.

8. Which team owns the longest winning streak in NBA history?

9. Wing defence, centre, goal defence and goal shooter are positions in which sport?

10. As of 2023, who holds the world record for highest football transfer fee?

11. Which former tennis player was the longest-serving presenter of BBC One's *A Question of Sport*?

12. Which former British sprinter has a stadium named after him in west London?

13. Lincoln City, Portsmouth, Ipswich Town and Shrewsbury Town all played in which football league during the 2022/23 season?

14. England's debut game at the 2022 World Cup saw five out of six goals scored by Black or mixed-race players. Who were the four scorers?

15. In which city will the 2024 Olympics be held?

A QUESTION OF SPORT

ROUND 2

1. Maro Itoje plays which sport?
2. In what year did Serena Williams first become ranked world number 1?
3. What footballer received an eight-month suspension by the FA for missing a drug test in 2003?
4. In what arena did Anthony Joshua face Jarrell Miller on 1 June 2019?
5. How is football player Edson Arantes do Nascimento better known?
6. What is the name of the implement needed to hit the ball in snooker or pool?
7. Which nation has produced the most Formula One World Championship-winning drivers?
8. Shoulder roll, peek-a-boo and the clinch are all moves you would find in which sport?
9. Which country is Olympic gold medallist Caster Semenya from?
10. Which of the following basketball players have not dated a Kardashian or Jenner? Blake Griffin, James Harden and Russell Westbrook?
11. In what year did a handball from Luis Suárez and a missed penalty from Asamoah Gyan send Ghana home in the World Cup quarter-finals?
12. The Ashes series is played in which sport?

13. In 2019 BBC Sport was accused by bestselling co-author Yomi Adegoke of plagiarising what trademarked slogan?
14. Which popular manager said, 'I prefer not to speak, because if I speak I am in big trouble'?
15. The film *Cool Runnings* is based around which sport?

A QUESTION OF SPORT

ROUND 3

1. Who beat Venus Williams on the first day of Wimbledon 2019?
2. The Cricket World Cup was hosted by England and Wales in 2019. Which country won the tournament?
3. Which country hosted the 2019 Women's World Cup?
4. In football, what does VAR stand for?
5. What archaeological relics in the West Bank are also the name of a wrestling move?
6. Which player scored the final goal during the 2019 African Cup of Nations semi-final between Nigeria and Algeria?
7. Capoeira is a type of which sport?
8. Dina Asher-Smith hit the headlines in 2019 after becoming the first British woman to win a major outdoors sprint title at the World Championships. Which race did she win gold in?
9. Which of the following footballers is the only one not to have scored more than 50 international goals? Robin van Persie, Samuel Eto'o, Thierry Henry and Wayne Rooney.
10. I was the fourth draft pick in 1991, I started my career at Denver Nuggets and I've won NBA Defensive Player of the Year four times. Who am I?
11. In April 2019, Jamie Carragher and Gary Neville famously walked away from which female presenter in a pre-match awkward-camera-angle incident?
12. Which football team did Sol Campbell manage during the 2019/20 season?

13. Who is the only player in the WNBA to have won both Rookie of the Year and MVP in the same season?
14. The Barani, Randolph and Rudolph are moves found in which sport?
15. Which team did Cristiano Ronaldo play for when he scored his first professional goal?

A QUESTION OF SPORT

ROUND 4

1. How is the 1975 fight between Muhammed Ali and Joe Frazier better known?
2. What country does tennis player Naomi Osaka represent?
3. In what sport might you compete for the Claret Jug?
4. In what year did Maradona's Hand of God goal help send England home from the quarter-final of the World Cup?
5. Which ESPN sports commentator said the following: 'If you don't like it, don't watch me. I don't have to do it. I have a radio show, a TV show and a column. I don't need to do that.'
6. In 2019 South Africa won the Rugby World Cup. How many tries did Makazole Mapimpi score in the tournament?
7. Following an investigation by the FA, which female England player received an out-of-court settlement of £80,000 in 2017?
8. My real name is Paul Michael Levesque, I am best known as a wrestler. I used to be known in the ring as Terra Ryzing. I have a son who is also a wrestler, known in the ring as Jake Jackson. Who am I?
9. What is the traditional dessert served at Wimbledon?
10. 'I am regarded as one of the greatest sprinters of all time. I am a two-time Olympic gold medallist and a five-time world champion in the 100 metres. After returning from maternity leave in 2020 I became the fastest mother in history. Who am I?'

11. Arsenal Football Club was founded in 1886 in which area of London?
12. Cristiano Ronaldo was quick to move two bottles of Coca-Cola away from himself during a Euro 2020 press conference. Which player did the opposite and told Coca-Cola to contact him, his representatives and Roc Nation?
13. In June 2021, who became the first woman to take home seven US all-round titles for gymnastics?
14. In football, what is the definition of a 'perfect hat-trick'?
15. Who became the first British woman to win two gold medals at the same games after winning both the 800m and 1,500m in the 2004 Olympics?

A QUESTION OF SPORT

ROUND 5

1. 'The Last Stylebender' is the stage name for which UFC star?
2. How many people on a team are allowed to shoot in a netball match? For an additional point, list the position(s).
3. Name the head coach of the East Los Angeles College Huskies featured in Netflix docuseries *Last Chance U: Basketball*.
4. Raheem Sterling's second England goal at Euro 2020 took place on which commemorative UK-observed holiday?
5. Name the first (and only) African-born WWE champion.
6. 'The Texas Rattlesnake' is the nickname for which WWE star?
7. How many NFL players per team play on the field?
8. @m10_official is the Instagram handle of which midfielder?
9. Which Zambian national scored two hat-tricks in two games at the 2020 Tokyo Olympics?
10. 'First change', 'golden duck' and 'dolly' are terms used in which sport?
11. In 2021 Greek basketball player Giannis Antetokounmpo won the NBA Finals MVP award. Who was the last non-American to win the award and what country were they from?
12. What country won the first ever football World Cup in 1930?
13. Yusra Mardini – the Olympic athlete who swam for 3 hours in the open sea after fleeing Syria – competed in which event at the 2020 Tokyo Olympics?
14. Which of these is *not* an Olympic event: darts, speed walking, skateboarding?
15. Which player signed for Arsenal from Juventus in August 1999 for £11 million?

A QUESTION OF SPORT

ROUND 6

1. The Hillsborough Disaster took place in which city?
2. Translate the title of the song 'Ramenez la coupe à a maison' into English.
3. Mo Salah surpassed which player to become the highest-scoring African player in Premier League history?
4. Who won the first ever BBC African Sports Personality of the Year award?
5. Where did the 2014 football World Cup take place?
6. The sons of two former British boxers were scheduled to fight each other in October 2022. What were their father's full names?
7. A 'duck', 'nil' and 'love' are alternative words for what in sport?
8. Leon Edwards knocked out Kamaru Usman in the fifth round of their MMA championship fight, crowning him with which title?
9. How many goals were scored in total in the Sidemen FC Vs YouTube All-Stars that took place in September 2022?
10. What was the first video to ever reach 1 million views on YouTube?
11. In what year did Colin Kaepernick first take the knee?
12. TMZ released footage of NBA player Draymond Green punching which player during practice?
13. What is the ex-Nigerian football legend Taribo West's current profession?
14. What is the closest tube station to Tottenham Hotspur Stadium in London?
15. What is the opening move in tennis or badminton called?

A QUESTION OF SPORT

ROUND 7

1. What is the name of the top French football league?
2. Megan Rapinoe is best known for playing which sport?
3. Which NBA team did Shaquille O'Neal spend the most years playing for?
4. Which country hosted the 2006 football World Cup?
5. In the London 2012 Olympics women's 100 metres, which American sprinter finished second?
6. Manchester United acquired Sir Alex Ferguson from which Scottish club?
7. The Merseyside derby takes place between which two football teams?
8. In 'Super Saturday' of the London 2012 Olympics, Team GB won three athletics gold medals in which events?
9. The 2023 Super Bowl was contested between which two teams?
10. What surface does the French Open in tennis take place on?
11. Who scored a hat-trick in the 2022 football World Cup final?
12. Billie Jean King is famous for what sport?
13. Which one of tennis's four grand slams is held on grass?
14. What are the most points in an English Premier League season without winning the title?
15. What country's football team did Nigeria defeat to win the gold medal at the 1996 Olympics?

A QUESTION OF SPORT

ROUND 8

1. In what year did the Premier League start?
2. Sue Bird, Diana Taurasi and Maya Moore all played for which famous college team?
3. What does NFL stand for?
4. What name is given to the New Zealand men's rugby union team?
5. Australian WNBA coach Sandy Brondello left the Phoenix Mercury to coach which WNBA team?
6. What was Alex Morgan's celebration at the 2019 World Cup after scoring against England?
7. Which country is hosting the 2024 men's Euros?
8. Which football team holds the record for the fewest points in a Premier League season?
9. What is the lowest numbers of points gained in a Premier League season?
10. How many Olympic gold medals has Mo Farah won?
11. What is the name of Nigerian international footballer Jay-Jay Okocha's footballing nephew?
12. Which country has won the most men's football World Cups?
13. In the 1992 Barcelona Olympics, which athlete's father came onto the track to help his son finish the race after he suffered a torn hamstring?
14. What does MVP stand for?
15. Who has scored the most goals for the England Lionesses?

A QUESTION OF SPORT

ROUND 9

1. In 2012, Jamaica won the men's 4 × 100 metres in a world-record time of 36.84 seconds. Name two out of the four athletes in the team who ran in the final.
2. In what year did Allyson Felix win her first 200 metres Olympic gold medal?
3. Wayne Rooney scored a hat-trick in his Champions League debut against which team?
4. The Bundesliga is the top football league in what country?
5. Who won the gold medal at the men's singles final at the London 2012 Olympics?
6. Tom Brady holds the record for the most Super Bowl wins as a player. How many times has he won?
7. The Bryan brothers competed in which sport?
8. Who gave Mike Tyson the first loss of his professional career?
9. Manchester City's famous 'Agueroooo' moment came against which team when City won the Premier League title in 2012?
10. What nationality is Andre De Grasse?
11. Who won the Golden Boot at the 2022 Football World Cup in Qatar?
12. Anthony Martial was bought by Manchester United from which French club?
13. What US football club does David Beckham co-own?
14. What does the WSL stand for?
15. In 2010 Man City signed Yaya Touré from which club?

A QUESTION OF SPORT

ROUND 10

1. The Denver Nuggets are based in which state?
2. Which team won the 2022 NWSL Championship?
3. What nationality is tennis player Kim Clijsters?
4. Wayne Rooney scored his famous bicycle kick at Old Trafford against which team?
5. I was born in Lebanon, played with Michael Jordan and have won nine NBA championships as player and coach. Who am I?
6. Out of the four tennis Grand Slams, how many are played on hard courts?
7. Which Jamaican female sprinter is often called the 'Pocket Rocket'?
8. Which team has won Scotland's top-flight league championship the most times?
9. How many minutes do an NBA game last?
10. The NFL consists of how many clubs in total?
11. Tennis's US Open is held in which state?
12. The women's Euro 2022 final took place at Wembley Stadium between England and who?
13. What is the maximum roster size in the WNBA?
14. The Valley is the home of which English football club?
15. Which tennis player holds the record for the most French Open men's singles titles?

A QUESTION OF SPORT

ROUND 11

1. Which English football club did Nigerian international Nwankwo Kanu play the most games for in his career?
2. In the Tokyo 2020 Olympics women's 100 metres sprint, which nation made a clean sweep of the medals?
3. Allen Iverson spent most of his career with which team?
4. What are the two conferences in the NBA?
5. How many Champions League winners' medals does Gareth Bale have?
6. What two events did Usain Bolt specialise in?
7. In bowling, what is the name given for three consecutive strikes?
8. Which artist performed at the 2023 Super Bowl halftime show?
9. What term denotes a 40–40 scoreline in tennis?
10. How many Formula One championships did Michael Schumacher win?
11. Goodison Park is located in which UK city?
12. Which men's player has won the most Australian Open men's singles titles in the Open era?
13. Kobe Bryant was 13th overall draft pick in 1996. Which team was he selected by before being immediately traded to the Los Angeles Lakers?
14. Which cricketer has the nickname 'Little Master'?
15. Outside of sprinting, which other athletics event did Blessing Okagbare compete in?

A QUESTION OF SPORT

ROUND 12

1. 'Rumble in the Jungle' was an iconic fight in 1974 between which two heavyweight boxers?
2. In what year did Arsenal finish the season unbeaten, often referred to as the 'Invincibles season'?
3. Which Grand Slam did Serena Williams win while pregnant?
4. Three players hold the Premier League record for picking up the most red cards (8): Richard Dunne, Duncan Ferguson and who?
5. Who won Player of the Tournament in the 2022 football World Cup?
6. Brothers Alistair and Jonny Brownlee compete in which event?
7. Liverpool bought Jordan Henderson from which Premier League club?
8. Der Klassiker, the Bundesliga equivalent of Spain's El Clásico, takes place between which two teams?
9. Which player won the Ballon d'Or Féminin twice in a row in 2021 and 2022?
10. Who was the first Black woman to be ranked world No. 1 in the Open era by the Women's Tennis Association?
11. In 1993, which of these international superstars headlined the Super Bowl halftime show: Whitney Houston, Michael Jackson or Diana Ross?
12. To complete a career Golden Slam in tennis, one has to win all four Grand Slams and what else?

13. Who succeeded Arsène Wenger as manager of Arsenal?
14. In 2016, who became Formula One world champion and then announced his retirement from the sport five days later?
15. How many outfield players will be on a cricket field during a game?

A QUESTION OF SPORT

ROUND 13

1. In athletics, the longstanding women's 100 metres record is held by who?
2. Which team went unbeaten for an entire season in the Premier League?
3. As of 2023, which football player holds the record for the second-highest transfer fee?
4. Which tennis player won the women's singles at the London 2012 Olympics?
5. In 1994 an African team was ranked fifth in the FIFA rankings, the highest ever position for an African country. Which country was it?
6. Which football team's home ground is the Stadium of Light?
7. Which famous women's basketball coach took charge of college team UConn in 1985?
8. Which British tennis player went on to host *A Question of Sport*?
9. Which football team's home ground is the Bernabeu?
10. What is Michael Jordan's iconic jersey number?
11. Maria Sharapova is famous for which sport?
12. The nickname 'Bad Boys' was given to what NBA team in the 1980s?
13. Who is the Premier League record holder for assists?
14. Which of these names was not a #1 WNBA Draft pick: Candace Parker, Sylvia Fowles, Sue Bird?
15. The Vince Lombardi Trophy is awarded to the winning team of what sporting competition?

A QUESTION OF SPORT

ROUND 14

1. In which season did Leicester win the Premier League?
2. Jade Jones won Olympic gold in 2012 in which sport?
3. In basketball, if you add together the number of starters on a team plus the number of seconds on a standard possession shot clock, what do you get?
4. What is the name of Leeds United's home ground?
5. Which two countries co-hosted the African Cup of Nations in 2000?
6. Two NBA teams are tied for the most championships. One is the Los Angeles Lakers. What is the other team?
7. Who has been the most successful footballing country in women's World Cup history?
8. In his senior career, how many different clubs did Wayne Rooney play for?
9. Jackie Robinson was the first Black player to professionally play what sport?
10. What Olympic sport does Charlotte Dujardin compete in?
11. The all-German 2013 Champions League final between Bayern and Dortmund ended in what scoreline?
12. Harry Kane and Wayne Rooney are the top two goal scorers for the England men's national team. Which player comes next on the list?
13. The M23 derby takes place between which two football teams?
14. Which two teams did José Mourinho win the Champions League with?
15. Andy Murray has been to the final five times but never won which Grand Slam?

A QUESTION OF SPORT

ROUND 15

1. How many teams compete in the NBA?
2. Primeira Liga is the top football division in what country?
3. Who is Australia's top international goal scorer in men's football?
4. In 2019 Kawhi Leonard sent the Toronto Raptors to the Eastern Final with a dramatic Game 7 buzzer beater. Who were their opponents?
5. Which three players shared the Premier League Golden Boot in the 2018/19 season?
6. Lionel Messi went from Barcelona to which team in 2021?
7. Who succeeded Steph Houghton as captain of the England Lionesses?
8. The Europa League is a competition played in which sport?
9. Which football team's home ground is the Allianz Arena?
10. Who is Sweden's top international goal scorer in men's football ?
11. How many points are awarded to Formula One Grand Prix winners?
12. In what year did Roman Abramovich buy Chelsea?
13. Who was the first men's player to win five Champions League titles?
14. What country does Shaunae Miller-Uibo represent?
15. Steph Curry, Blake Griffin, James Harden and Jrue Holiday were all Round 1 draft picks in 2009. Who was selected first?

A QUESTION OF SPORT

ROUND 16

1. Which English football club did England manager Gareth Southgate play the most games for?
2. How many games does each NBA team play in the regular season?
3. What is the biggest Premier League home win to date?
4. Who did Serena Williams overtake to move into second place on the all-time women's Grand Slam list?
5. The Old Firm derby takes place between which two football teams?
6. What does WWE stand for?
7. How many consecutive points must you win at a 40–40 scoreline in tennis to win the game?
8. Jessica Ennis-Hill competed in what event?
9. Who is the WSL top goal-scorer?
10. Who won Goalkeeper of the Tournament in the 2022 men's World Cup?
11. Which country won the 2021 Africa Cup of Nations (AFCON)?
12. How many times did Manchester United 'three-peat' under Alex Ferguson?
13. Between his two Chelsea stints, which two clubs did José Mourinho manage?
14. What nationality is football player Alex Morgan?
15. Who did José Mourinho call a 'specialist in failure'?

A QUESTION OF SPORT

ROUND 17

1. Who won Young Player of the Tournament in the 2022 World Cup?
2. Who succeeded Phil Neville as manager of England Lionesses?
3. The infamous Cantona kung-fu kick happened against which team?
4. Which team holds the record for the longest Premier League unbeaten away run?
5. In 2012 Leicester City signed striker Jamie Vardy for £1 million. Which club did they sign him from?
6. Name the two Welsh clubs that have played in the Premier League.
7. Who was the first man to complete a career Golden Slam in tennis?
8. As of 2023, which man holds the record for the most goals scored at World Cups?
9. What does WNBA stand for?
10. British athlete Christine Ohuruogu specialised in which event?
11. What are the two NBA teams based in Florida?
12. Which team has won the most games in Premier League history?
13. Which country knocked the England football team out of the Euro 2016?
14. Who won the final of the 2009 US Open men's singles?
15. Venus Williams won her first singles title at which Grand Slam?

A QUESTION OF SPORT

ROUND 18

1. Which football team's home ground is Anfield?
2. The French Open in tennis is staged in which city?
3. Which football team's home ground is Craven Cottage?
4. Which Scottish football club did Fraser Forster play for?
5. Germany and Italy are the joint most successful winners of the men's Euros. How many times have they both lifted the trophy?
6. The SheBelieves Cup is a tournament in which sport?
7. Centre, power-forward and point guard are three of the five on-court positions in basketball. Name the other two.
8. As of 2023, who are the only three Premier League players to have scored over 200 goals in the competition?
9. What tennis player holds the record for the most Australian Open women's singles wins?
10. The Stanley Cup is a trophy awarded in which sport?
11. Who is Steffi Graf's husband?
12. With which Formula One team did Sebastian Vettel win four consecutive Drivers' Championships between 2010 and 2013?
13. In 2011 Manchester United lost the Champions League final to Barcelona. What was the score?
14. The El Clásico derby takes place between which two teams?
15. NBA's Golden State Warriors are based in which US state?

A QUESTION OF SPORT

ROUND 19

1. When Leicester won the Premier League in the 2015/16 season, who was their top scorer?
2. Who was the first Italian manager to win the Premier League?
3. Which country has won the Africa Cup of Nations the most times?
4. Dallas Mavericks shooting guard Luka Dončić is from which country?
5. Kevin Durant won two NBA championships with which team?
6. Kye Whyte from Peckham won an Olympic silver for Team GB in 2020 in what new event?
7. Athlete Louis Smith is famous for competing in which specific gymnastics event?
8. 'The Springboks' is the name given to what country's rugby team?
9. Which country hosted the 2010 football World Cup?
10. Which GB women's athlete holds the British record for both the 100 metres and 200 metres?
11. 2022 MVP pick Nikola Jokić is from which country?
12. What does NFL stand for?
13. Who was the first GB female gymnast to win a medal at the European Championships, World Championships and Olympic Games?
14. Which football team's home ground is Selhurst Park?
15. In what month is tennis's Australian Open usually held?

A QUESTION OF SPORT

ROUND 20

1. Who was the Golden Boot winner at the Women's Euros 2022?
2. Which player holds the record for the fastest hat-trick in the Premier League?
3. Before Andy Murray, who was the last British tennis player to win a men's singles Grand Slam tournament?
4. As of 2023, how many WNBA teams are in the league?
5. Which women's football team does Natalie Portman have shares in?
6. Which player has scored the most hat-tricks in the WSL?
7. Since 2004, the Super Bowl has been played in what month?
8. Which player holds the record for the most NBA championships?
9. What is Cristiano Ronaldo's iconic shirt number?
10. What time did Usain Bolt get in the 2008 Olympics in the 100 metres to break the world record?
11. Which men's player is Liverpool's all-time top goal-scorer?
12. Kyrie Irving was born in which country?
13. What football team is Ryan Reynolds a co-owner of?
14. Who was the inaugural Premier League Golden Boot winner?
15. In what sport did Luke Campbell win a gold in the London 2012 Olympics?

A QUESTION OF SPORT

ROUND 21

1. Which basketball star had the nickname 'The Black Mamba'?
2. Which two clubs have Thomas Tuchel and Jürgen Klopp both managed?
3. Mike Tyson bit off part of whose ear in 1997?
4. In which sport is 180 deemed a perfect score?
5. Michael Jordan spent most of his career at which team?
6. Which Premier League goalkeeper holds the record for the most clean sheets?
7. Two teams have the most Super Bowl titles: the New England Patriots and who?
8. Which WSL team has won the most titles?
9. Against what team did Ole Gunnar Solskjær score four goals in 12 minutes?
10. How many teams has LeBron James won an NBA championship with? Give the number and the teams.
11. A men's singles Grand Slam tennis match is the best of how many sets?
12. Which team in the Premier League was deducted points in the 1996/97 season?
13. Which darts player has the nickname 'The Power'?
14. Luke Shaw, Gareth Bale and Theo Walcott all came from which club's academy?
15. In which film might you find someone wearing a hoodie with a logo saying EHS to support their school team?

4

MUSIC

Calling all music connoisseurs and 'I love this song' merchants! This category should be a walk in the park. The answers can be found on page 271.

GUESS THE SONG

ROUND 1
Play each song for 15 seconds

1. 50 Cent – 'Many Men'
2. Travis Scott – 'Goosebumps'
3. The Weeknd – 'Often'
4. Brent Faiyaz – 'Clouded'
5. Bill Withers – 'Lean on Me'
6. Gyptian – 'Wine Slow'
7. Michael Jackson – 'Billie Jean'
8. Busted – 'Year 3000'
9. Kelly Clarkson – 'Because of You'
10. Runtown – 'Mad Over You'
11. Mavado – 'So Special'
12. Adele – 'Love in the Dark'
13. MJ Cole, Elisabeth Troy – 'Crazy Love'
14. Bow Wow, T-Pain, Johntá Austin – 'Outta My System'
15. Tink – 'Treat Me Like Somebody'
16. Soul for Real – 'Candy Rain'
17. Potter Payper – 'Gangsteritus'
18. Deee-Lite – 'Groove Is in the Heart'
19. Yungen, Yxng Bane – 'Bestie'
20. Tevin Campbell – 'Can We Talk'
21. Headie One – 'Both'
22. Big Brovaz – 'Nu flow'
23. Jazmine Sullivan – 'Bust Your Windows'
24. Kandi – 'Don't Think I'm Not'
25. Donae'o – 'Devil in a Blue Dress'

GUESS THE SONG

ROUND 2
Play each song for 10 seconds

1. Asake – 'Terminator'
2. Jamelia – 'Thank You'
3. JME, Giggs – 'Man Don't Care'
4. Beyoncé – 'Heated'
5. Wretch 32 – 'Traktor'
6. Nao – 'Drive and Disconnect'
7. Britney Spears – 'Sometimes'
8. Miley Cyrus – 'The Climb'
9. Midnight Crew – 'Igwe'
10. Stormzy – 'Hide & Seek'
11. SZA, Travis Scott – 'Love Galore'
12. Burna Boy, Popcaan – 'Toni-Ann Singh
13. Kojo Funds, RAYE – 'Check'
14. Vybz Kartel – 'Business'
15. Mariah Carey – 'We Belong Together'
16. Usher – 'U Remind Me'
17. Liberty X – 'Just a Little'
18. Future – 'March Madness'
19. Crystal Waters – 'Gypsy Woman'
20. Santi, Shane Eagle, Tomi Agape and Amaarae – 'Rapid Fire'
21. Drake – 'Marvins Room'
22. Artful Dodger – 'Movin' Too Fast'
23. Evelyn 'Champagne' King – 'Love Come Down'
24. N-Dubz – 'I Swear'
25. NSG – 'Petite'

GUESS THE SONG

ROUND 3
Play each song for 5 seconds

1. Angel – 'Shaggy'
2. Sarkodie, Bisa Kdei – 'Chingam'
3. Jennifer Lopez – 'Love Don't Cost a Thing'
4. Pheelz, Buju – 'Finesse'
5. ZieZie – 'Fine Girl'
6. Tinie Tempah – 'Pass Out'
7. Blackstreet – 'No Diggity'
8. Sanchez – 'Frenzy'
9. Mary J. Blige – 'I Can Love You'
10. Gyptian – 'Non Stop'
11. PARTYNEXTDOOR – 'Not Nice'
12. Ruff-N-Smooth – 'Swagger'
13. Tosin Martins – 'Olo Mi'
14. Lloyd, Lil Wayne – 'You'
15. Ja Rule, Ashanti – 'Mesmerize'
16. Cassie – 'Long Way 2 Go'
17. Jay-Z, Beyoncé – '03 Bonnie & Clyde'
18. Donell Jones, Lisa 'Left-Eye' Lopes – 'You Know What's Up'
19. Eve, Gwen Stefani – 'Let Me Blow Ya Mind'
20. Krept & Konan – 'Don't Waste My Time'
21. Doja Cat, Saweetie – 'Best Friend'
22. The Script – 'The Man Who Can't Be Moved'
23. Olamide, Bad Boy Timz – 'Loading'
24. Dizzee Rascal – 'Fix Up, Look Sharp'
25. Nu Brand Flexxx – 'Gash by da Hour'

GUESS THE SONG

ROUND 4
Play each song for 3 seconds

1. Giggs – 'You Raised Me'
2. Destiny's Child – 'Girl'
3. JoJo – 'Leave (Get Out)'
4. Rihanna – 'Take a Bow'
5. J Hus – 'Did You See'
6. Wizkid – 'No Lele'
7. J Hus, DoccyDocs – 'Lean & Bop'
8. Nicki Minaj – 'Itty Bitty Piggy'
9. Diddy, Christina Aguilera – 'Tell Me'
10. Lotto Boyz – 'No Don'
11. Gunna – '25K Jacket'
12. Vybz Kartel – 'Fever'
13. Maleek Berry, WizKid – 'The Matter'
14. Usher, Alicia Keys – 'My Boo'
15. Beyoncé – 'Check on It'
16. Stormzy – 'WickedSkengMan 4'
17. Kojo Funds – 'My 9ine'
18. Young Thug – 'Check'
19. Davido – 'IF'
20. DJ Pied Piper – 'Do You Really Like It?'
21. T2, Jodie Aysha – 'Heartbroken'
22. 50 Cent – '21 Questions'
23. Lil Uzi Vert – 'Just Wanna Rock'
24. Kes – 'Hello'
25. Rihanna – 'If It's Lovin' That You Want'

UK GARAGE ROUND

1. Name the Southampton-based duo with seven consecutive UK Top 20 singles from 1999 to 2001.
2. MCs are a staple of any garage party. What does 'MC' stand for?
3. Producer Nathan Gerald is better known as who?
4. In which London venue was the first UK Garage Fest held?
5. Garage duo Joel Samuel and Michael Rose are known by what stage name?
6. What year did The Streets release their single 'Has It Come to This?'?
7. Name the popular garage night in the 1990s with a Sunday residency at London nightclub The End.
8. Which song did both Katy B and Ms. Dynamite appear on together?
9. Name the UK garage collective behind the hit song 'Champagne Dance'.
10. What was the first UK garage song to reach number 1 in the UK charts? Both song and artist are needed.
11. How many members formed the group Heartless Crew?
12. Which American music genre was UK garage heavily inspired by?
13. Name the garage song that shares a similar title with a popular Beyoncé song. Both song and artist are needed.
14. Which two genres are said to have emerged from garage in the UK?
15. UK garage act 3 of a Kind are best known for their 2004 number 1 hit single titled what?

GRIME ROUND

1. What was the name of Wiley's first album?
2. The diss track 'Listen Likkle Man' was directed at which artist?
3. In a grime context, what does LOTM stand for?
4. Flowdan, Danny Weed, Tinchy Stryder, Tania Foster and DJ Maximum have all been a part of which Grime collective?
5. Dizzee Rascal's 2003 album *Boy in da Corner* won him which prestigious award?
6. What is the widely accepted tempo in BPM of a grime beat?
7. How much did Skepta say his MOBO-winning video for 'That's Not Me' cost?
8. What is the name of the instrumental used in both Stormzy's 'WickedSkengman Part 3' and 'Thiago Silva' by Dave and AJ Tracey?
9. In a clash with Bashy, Ghetts says he was a bad boy in jail. Who is the person named who he claims can verify this?
10. Who wrote the book *Grime Kids*?
11. Which MC always references their 'apnas' and 'karlas' in their singles and freestyles?
12. 'Tough yat like me can make a bredda cry' is a line from which artist's 2011 YouTube freestyle?
13. Which public location does Chip choose for his diss tracks?
14. Skepta's diss track 'Nasty' is directed at which MC?
15. Tyrone Mark Lindo is the full name of which MC turned TV personality?

5

CULTURE

Ears to the ground? In the know? This chapter will really test your knowledge across film, TV, music, fashion and more! The answers can be found on pages 272–277.

POP CULTURE ROUND

1. Name Tracee Ellis Ross's character in hit sitcom *Black-ish*.
2. 'I Wish I Missed My Ex', 'Simmer' and 'What You Did' are songs from which album by what artist?
3. Who is the most followed person on Instagram?
4. What is the name of Monica and Brandy's hit duet?
5. In the 2000s No Fear was a popular what?
6. As of January 2023, how many seasons of *RuPaul's Drag Race* have there been?
7. What are the first names of Kourtney Kardashian's children?
8. CeeLo Green is one half of which duo?
9. In which UK city is the TV series *Coronation Street* set?
10. In November 2022 two TV anchors were exposed after it was revealed they were having an extramarital relationship with each other. What morning TV show were they hosts of?
11. Anne Robinson is the long-standing host of which TV game show?
12. Calvin Broadus Jr is better known as who?
13. It was announced in January 2023 that London-based streetwear brand Corteiz is launching its first major brand collaboration with who?
14. 'Bluku!' and 'bud-a-bup-bup' are which grime artist's catchphrases?
15. Dappy, Tulisa and Fazer make up which UK musical group?

FILM AND TV

ROUND 1

1. The Netflix documentary *Making a Murderer* details the trial of which Wisconsin man?
2. Ncuti Gatwa, Gillian Anderson and Asa Butterfield star in which hit Netflix show?
3. *The Crown* explores the life of Queen Elizabeth II and her family. Why did the Queen's uncle abdicate the throne?
4. In the anime series *The Seven Deadly Sins*, what move did Meliodas use to defeat the Holy Knight Guila in Necropolis?
5. Adjoa Andoh plays what character in *Bridgerton*?
6. Which company is older, Netflix or Google?
7. Randall, Kate, Kevin and Rebecca are characters in which hit show?
8. In the film *Shark Tale*, what type of sea creatures were Bert & Ernie?
9. In which country does Monica play basketball after college in the romantic classic *Love & Basketball*?
10. Name the *EastEnders* barmaid who, although she rarely speaks, has been working in the Queen Vic since the show started.
11. 'Here's a nice normal girl in an ordinary world' is the opening line for which childhood TV show?
12. On the TV series *Insecure*, what was the name of Issa's first workplace?
13. Which actor played Linda in the film *Pursuit of Happyness*?
14. In the film *Get Out*, what was the name of the otherworldly purgatory Black people got trapped in.
15. The phrase 'Damn, double homicide' is from which reality TV show?

FILM AND TV

ROUND 2

1. Mahershala Ali became the first Muslim actor to win an Academy Award for his role in what film?
2. Cameron Tucker, Manny Delgado and Mitchell Pritchett are all characters from which popular television series?
3. What year did Maya Jama take over as the British *Love Island* host?
4. Name both protagonists in *Love Jones*, giving the full names of both characters.
5. Who won *The Celebrity Circle* series for Stand Up to Cancer in 2021?
6. In January 2023, *Girls Trip* screenwriter Tracy Oliver confirmed a *Girls Trip* sequel set in which country?
7. Name the Black British actor who played PC Lewis Hardy in the ITV series *The Bill*.
8. Who does Lupita Nyong'o play in *Black Panther*?
9. Which reality dating series uses modern technology to help people find love as 20-plus single men and women try to find their perfect matches?
10. Which US state is the movie *Fruitvale Station* set in?
11. Comedy panel show *Don't Hate the Playaz* is screened on which channel?
12. Ruby's, Angie's Den & Scarlet R&R are the names for a club featured where?
13. What does *TOWIE* stand for?
14. What year was the film *Belly* released?
15. *Baby Driver*, *Miami Vice* and *Dreamgirls* all have which actor in common?

FILM AND TV

ROUND 3

1. What is the name of the film and TV studio located in Bow, east London?
2. Who directed the film *Poetic Justice* released in 1993?
3. Who played the lead role in the 2004 movie *Bullet Boy*?
4. In *Game of Thrones*, what is the name of the former slave turned trusted advisor to Daenerys?
5. Will Smith rejected the offer to be the lead role in which 1999 sci-fi film?
6. What does BAFTA stand for?
7. Name the 1990s classic that featured Angela Bassett, Whitney Houston, Lela Rochon and Loretta Devine as the lead roles.
8. The film *Rye Lane* is set in which two parts of London?
9. Who was the first Black British actor to be nominated for the Best Actor Academy Award for his role in the film *12 Years a Slave*?
10. The series of novels-turned-TV drama *The No. 1 Ladies' Detective Agency* was screened on which channel?
11. John Witherspoon is the actor that voices which character in *The Boondocks*?
12. In 2022 Surrey-based Shepperton film studio announced an expansion. Which two companies have committed to leasing studio space for future projects?
13. Daniel Kaluuya is the second Black British actor to be nominated for Best Actor at the Academy Awards for his role in which film?

14. The BRIT School is a performing and creative arts school located in Croydon. What is the minimum age a pupil can be to attend the school?
15. Suzanne Packer is known for playing Tess Bateman in which BBC medical drama?

ANIME ROUND

1. In the anime *Boku No Hero* (*My Hero Academia*), what is Gran Torino's quirk?
2. What is the name of the character that leads the Blue Lock Project?
3. What's the name of the principal from *Boku No Hero* (*My Hero Academia*)?
4. In the anime *Blue Lock*, what is the name given to Yoichi Isagi and his team?
5. How many strikers start in the anime *Blue Lock*?
6. In the anime *Sword Art Online*, what date was the Sword Art Online VR MMORPG game release?
7. In the anime *Ao Ashi*, what is the name of the youth team that Ashito Aoi plays for?
8. In the anime *Boku No Hero* (*My Hero Academia*), before losing his fit to Overhaul, what quirk did Mirio Togata have?
9. In *DBZ*, what is used to recoup a character's strength?
10. One year in the Hyperbolic Time Chamber is equivalent to how much time in the real world?
11. Who was the winner of the U.A. Sports Festival Arc?
12. Which Titan is known for their stamina?
13. What club is Mob in *Mob Psycho 100* a part of?
14. In *Spy Family*, what is Anya's favourite cartoon show?
15. Which anime features an arms dealer and her body guards?

MARVEL ROUND

1. In *Black Panther 2*, what is the reason given for T'Challa's death?
2. Which university did Tony Stark graduate from?
3. How many infinity stones are there?
4. Which Marvel film does Elon Musk appear in?
5. What are the names of Thanos's adopted daughters?
6. What is the nickname of Captain America's best friend?
7. Which villain exposes Peter Parker's identity as Spiderman in *Spider-Man: Far From Home*?
8. Which eye does Nick Fury wear his eye-patch over?
9. In *Black Panther 2*, who voices Shuri's A.I., Griot?
10. How did Bruce Banner become the Incredible Hulk?
11. What is the name of Thor's sister?
12. Which actor plays Killmonger in the *Black Panther* movies?
13. Which superhero gives their life to kill Thanos?
14. What is Captain America's shield made of?
15. Which Avenger cuts off Thanos's head?

FASHION ROUND

1. Fisayo Longe is the owner of which contemporary fashion brand?
2. I am a Liberian-American fashion designer. The likes of Swae Lee, Alexandria Ocasio-Cortez and Beyoncé have been spotted in my designs, and I recently collaborated with UGG. Who am I?
3. H&M collaborated with which designer brand in 2018?
4. Which shoe brand saw a soaring rise in sales and experienced a website crash after Nicki Minaj posted a picture wearing a pair in May 2021?
5. What is the official name of the trainer popularly known as 110s?
6. Who founded the American clothing brand Rocawear?
7. Name the online marketplace and clothing reseller, primarily of trainers.
8. Which fashion house logo depicts a polo player on a horse?
9. Exaggerated baby hair, big gold hoops, dummies and which edible item were branded the 2000s British teenage uniform?
10. British designer Wales Bonner first collaborated with which sportswear giant in 2020?
11. In which cities are the four major fashion weeks held?
12. What was the price of the Air Force 1 trainer when they were first released?
13. How is a diamond-encrusted watch sometimes described in the Black community?

14. Dsquared2 is considered to be one of the world's most popular and luxurious fashion brands. In which country was it founded?

15. Pharrell Williams and Nigo founded streetwear label BBC in 2003. What does BBC stand for?

WHO AM I?

ROUND 1

1. Formally known as Jermaine Sinclair Scott, I am a singer, songwriter and rapper from north London. My latest venture is into the world of CBD oils. Six words from me might read: 'I found my treasure in you.'

2. I was the England women's football manager from 1998 until 2013, and its youngest ever coach. An OBE and MBE holder, I am a tremendous ambassador for women in football.

3. My favourite drink is a brandy and Coke. I've been a rapper in the UK scene for a long time, but I'm Still Sittin' Here.

4. OG YouTube legend, but I started my career in finance. Known for my beauty, fashion and lifestyle content, you might find me on my new channel The Break!

5. Amin Mohamed is my birth name. I am a comedian and social media personality with an infectious laugh. I am a member of the Beta Squad but am mainly known for missing a Soccer Aid match penalty in 2020.

6. An enslaved man brought to freedom, I am best known for my campaign to abolish the slave trade. I was given the name Gustavus Vassa and my autobiography helped influence the Slave Trade Act of 1807, which abolished the African slave trade in Britain.

7. In 1964 I walked into a pub in Bristol and ordered a half pint when it was legal for pubs to refuse Black people service. I organised the bus boycott in Bristol and in 2008 I was made Freeman of the same city.

8. Some might refer to me as the most recognised broadcaster in British history. I am of Trinidadian-British heritage, my biography is titled *An Improbable Life* and you may have first seen me on the *News at Ten*.

9. I am part of one of the best-known Black British families of this time. I am a cultural curator and share on the internet (if you trust it) my Top 5 favourite artists.

10. Hailing from Wolverhampton, I am a retired team GB field athlete, I won the gold medal in the heptathlon at the 2000 Sydney Olympics and bronze at the 1996 Atlanta Olympics. I am now a regular pundit on the BBC.

11. In my own words, 'An actor, MC and now I'm rakin'.' I am also an executive producer. You might find me on Summerhouse Estate.

12. My money don't jiggle jiggle, it folds.

13. I was nominated for an Academy Award as Best Supporting Actress for my role as Tatiana in *Hotel Rwanda*. I am Nigerian-Jewish and most recently starred in *Raymond & Ray* and *Death on the Nile*.

14. I am an English professional footballer who was one of the first Black players in British football after the Second World War. I later became Britain's first well-known Black stand-up comedian.

15. I am a dancer and music artist, known for making viral music on TikTok. I ain't never been with a baddie.

WHO AM I?

ROUND 2

1. Formally known as Justin Clarke, I am a grime MC and was a member of NASTY crew. I can make anyone sing for me.

2. I am a grime legend, Bluku bluku! Out of all my iconic moments on the scene, one of my favourites was my appearance in Ikea's 2019 Christmas advert.

3. I am one of the most successful British female music artists in history. I have a soulful and jazzy sound, but a deeply English quality that makes me hard to categorise. I might give you a Kiss of Life.

4. I am a legendary British music entrepreneur and the creator of SB.TV.

5. I am a Crawley-born rapper, author and activist; my biggest hit was named after the greatest English playwright of all time, and I also have a production company that features his name.

6. I am a football player by profession and am known for my campaign to feed impoverished children during their half-term.

7. I am a British entrepreneur and the founder of the Music of Black Origin (MOBO) awards.

8. I was the first Black Briton to study at Harvard Law School. I am a politician, and at the time of writing I am the Shadow Secretary of State for Foreign, Commonwealth and Development Affairs.

9. I am the oldest sprinter to win the men's 100 metres Olympic title. My international career spanned 17 years,

during which I competed over 60 times for this country and won more major championship medals than any other British male sprinter.

10. I am a Birmingham-born ex-professional footballer-turned-pundit. Playing at right-back, I helped Manchester City win their first league title in 44 years. Now I host Sky Sports.

11. Hailing from Birmingham, I initially found fame on Season 3 of *Big Brother*. I am best known for my showbiz segment on ITV's *This Morning*, where I infamously pushed a sailor weatherman into a river by mistake!

12. I wrote the books *White Teeth*, *Swing Time* and *The Autograph Man*.

13. You might have found me in my headscarf ranting on Instagram, and I have since amassed a huge following for my strong opinions and no-nonsense social commentary. I have my own self-titled show!

14. I am a Ghanaian British rapper and you might have heard me on Channel U back in the day. Also known as a Star in the Hood, my favourite pick-up line is 'There's Something About Your Smile'.

15. Born in Stockport, Greater Manchester, I am a British television and radio presenter, best known for presenting on BBC Radio 1Xtra from 2012 to 2021.

TWITTER AND TIKTOK ROUND

1. Name the 2020 film based on a 2015 viral Twitter thread.

2. Between 2012 and 2017, which day of the week had the highest chance of Twitter beef?

3. Popular sex and relationship expert Oloni is well known for her threads made from anonymous stories. What is the question she starts her viral threads with?

4. Which Black songwriter from Streatham rose to prominence after one of her songs gained huge popularity on TikTok in 2022?

5. In 2020, Black people were going to reportedly receive superpowers on which date?

6. What was TikTok formerly known as?

7. UK Black Twitter often uses two terms to refer to our French counterparts on the site. One is Baguette Twitter, what is the other?

8. What does NPC stand for?

9. Name the feature that Twitter introduced in 2022 that enables you to tweet to a smaller audience of your choice.

10. TikTok channel @hopelessromanticsociety conducts street-style interviews across New York on which topic?

11. A viral TikTok video of an excerpt from a sermon shows a Ghanaian pastor stating that the best Valentine's gift you can give a woman is what?

12. Which two celebrities had Twitter beef, where one screen-shotted the other's net worth and put it in their header photo?

13. Born from Clubhouse, name the Twitter space hosted by Ashleigh Louise that discusses hot topics in the Black community?

14. What kind of content does viral TikToker Keith Lee create?

15. Between 2022 and 2023, TikTok hair trends heavily influenced the Black girl community to dye their hair which colour?

MY WIFE AND KIDS

ROUND 1

1. How many seasons are there in the hit TV series *My Wife and Kids*?
2. What is the unexpected cliffhanger at the end of the final episode of the entire series?
3. At what age did Jay get pregnant with Junior?
4. Which actor originally played the role of Vanessa?
5. The character Roger in Season 1 is replaced, although played by the same actor, by who?
6. What is Michael Kyle's business?
7. In one episode, Kady eats something belonging to Michael, and in return the three kids are forced to eat it for breakfast, lunch and dinner. What is it?
8. What was Franklin's sister called on the show?
9. What is Jay's middle name?
10. What is the name of the family who opened a restaurant across the street and tried to put Jay's Soul Kitchen out of business?
11. Which dance move does Michael perform during his dance-off with Bobby Shaw?
12. What is Franklin's middle name?
13. What was Kady's school play?
14. What is the name of the couple's therapist on the show?
15. What is the title of the poem that begins, 'Open the door, close the door, I am so confused'?

6

HISTORY

A not so typical Black history quiz covering the world. You may also surprise yourself and learn something new! The answers can be found on pages 277–288.

BLACK HISTORY

ROUND 1

1. In what year did the Bristol Bus Boycott take place?
2. Who said the following: 'Darkness cannot drive out darkness: only light can do that.'
3. Who was the first Black woman to host ITV's *News at 10*?
4. Lavinya Stennett created which initiative for social change in schools?
5. Joshua Beckford, at age six, became the youngest person to do what?
6. Phyllis Opoku-Gyimah, also known as Lady Phyll, is the co-founder of which UK-based event and social enterprise?
7. Which sub-Saharan African country was the first to gain freedom from colonial rule?
8. #SayHerName is a movement created specifically after the death of who?
9. Where did the *Empire Windrush* dock?
10. In the song 'Mel Made Me Do It', what did Stormzy say the 'M' on his hairline stands for?
11. What is the only city in the UK that Martin Luther King visited outside of London?
12. Which 18th-century Black campaigner for the abolition of slavery is commemorated at 73 Riding House Street, Marylebone?
13. Bobby Seale and Huey P. Newton founded which political party?
14. Name the church in Liverpool where many settlers from West Africa, the Caribbean and America were baptised.
15. *A Movement Not a Moment* is a mural in Bristol created by who?

BLACK HISTORY

ROUND 2

1. Who was the first Black player to be picked for the England national football team but never played for them?
2. What was the name of the song sampled in 'One Dance' by Drake? Both song title and artist are needed.
3. Name the first Black British author to top the UK's bestsellers list since records began in 1998?
4. Who designed Stormzy's Union Jack bulletproof vest for his Glastonbury performance?
5. In what year did Nigeria gain independence from the UK?
6. Which rugby league side did Dwain Chambers play for in 2009?
7. Who is the author of the *Noughts & Crosses* series?
8. What is the name of the first TV show Michaela Coel created?
9. In what year did Channel U launch?
10. Which civil rights activist led the Bristol Bus Boycott of 1963?
11. Tony Collins took charge of which club to become the first Black manager in the English Football League?
12. From which area of London did grime originate?
13. Who is the author of *All Things Fall Apart*?
14. In what year did Stormzy headline Glastonbury?
15. In what year did Ghana gain independence from the UK?

BLACK HISTORY

ROUND 3

1. Who was the world's reportedly first Black professional football player?
2. Who wrote the play *For Black Boys Who Have Considered Suicide When the Hue Gets Too Heavy*?
3. Which TV show was centred around a barbershop in Peckham?
4. In what year was the TV show *Top Boy* first released?
5. What was the name of the Black nurse who treated the wounded in the Crimean War?
6. Which Black British actor first won an Oscar?
7. In what year did BET launch in the UK?
8. In whose basement did Lord of the Mic start?
9. Which famous soul singer's father played for Celtic?
10. In what year did Wizkid release his debut album?
11. Which British sprinter was belatedly awarded a silver medal in the 1988 Olympics?
12. Who is known as the father of Afrobeat?
13. In what year did Tessa Sanderson win Olympic gold in the javelin?
14. Who is the author of *Half of a Yellow Sun*?
15. Who is the fastest woman sprinter in British history?

BLACK HISTORY

ROUND 4

1. Who holds the British record for the high jump?
2. Who is popularly known as Britain's 'first Black queen'?
3. In which sport did Nicola Adams become the first woman to win an Olympic gold medal?
4. Who was the first Black female journalist to feature on British television?
5. On which TV channel did Trevor McDonald present the news?
6. In what year was *Kidulthood* released?
7. In what year was *Adulthood* released?
8. Who filmed, directed and wrote *Blue Story*?
9. John Barnes was born on which Caribbean island?
10. In what year did Jamaica gain independence from the UK?
11. What is the percentage of 'Black, Black British, Black Welsh, Caribbean or African' people in the UK according to the 2021 census?
12. Which Caribbean country was the first country to remove the British monarch as head of state?
13. In what year did Stormzy release *Gang Signs & Prayer*?
14. Who is the founder of Corteiz?
15. Who is the first Black female manager of any England national team?

BLACK HISTORY

ROUND 5

1. Which Black British make-up artist has been appointed a dame?
2. What is Bob Marley's full name?
3. Alice Dearing is the first Black woman to represent Britain in which event?
4. Which country colonised the Democratic Republic of the Congo?
5. In what year was Nelson Mandela released from prison?
6. Who is the founder of the digital magazine *Black Ballad*?
7. Which Black chef was a lead presenter on *Ready Steady Cook*?
8. In what year did James Peters become England's first Black rugby union player?
9. Who is known as the 'godfather of grime'?
10. Who is the first Black British lifestyle YouTuber to gain 1 million subscribers?
11. 'Worl' Boss' is a nickname for which artist?
12. In what year did Trinidad and Tobago gain independence?
13. In what year did Choice FM launch?
14. Who directed the film *12 Years a Slave*?
15. Horace Ové's film *Pressure* was released in what year?

BLACK HISTORY

ROUND 6

1. What was the name of the first president of the Republic of the Congo?
2. In what year did the Nigerian Civil War start?
3. Which song featuring an Afrobeat artist was the first to hit 1 billion streams on Spotify?
4. Brinsley Forde of Aswad starred in which 1980 cult classic?
5. Who is widely credited as the 'godfather of house music'?
6. *Burning an Illusion* was directed by which Black British filmmaker?
7. Which athlete has ten global championship gold medals?
8. In which Olympics did Dame Kelly Holmes win gold in two events?
9. Which sibling duo founded Boy Better Know?
10. Who is the editor-in-chief of British *Vogue*?
11. In what year did OBE TV launch in the UK.?
12. In what year did the first Notting Hill Carnival take place?
13. What is the name of the photographer who is also a co-founder of Choice FM?
14. Who are the co-founders of No Signal radio?
15. What was the name of the first Ghanaian president?

BLACK HISTORY

ROUND 7

1. Which Black British actor worked at Ford Dagenham?
2. Who is the first Black woman to be inducted into the British Hairdressing Hall of Fame?
3. The TV series *Insecure* launched in which year?
4. What was the name of the subscription UK TV channel that played African American TV shows?
5. In what year did So Solid Crew release '21 Seconds'?
6. Who is the editor-in-chief of *Elle UK*?
7. Which artist in the year 2000 became the youngest male artist to reach number 1 in the charts?
8. In what year was *Black Panther* released?
9. Who is the founder of the MOBO Awards?
10. In what year was slavery abolished in England?
11. Who is known as the wealthiest person in history?
12. In what year did the Sierra Leone Civil War start?
13. What was the former national capital of Nigeria?
14. Who was the first female self-made millionaire in America?
15. As of February 2023, which artist has 32 Grammys?

BLACK HISTORY

ROUND 8

1. What date is the Democratic Republic of Congo's Independence Day?
2. Name one of the three co-founders of GRM Daily.
3. Who was the first Black person to win an Oscar?
4. Who was the first Black man to ever win an Oscar?
5. Who is the author of *Giovanni's Room*?
6. What is the name of the all-female tribe in *The Woman King*?
7. Which British DJ helped push Afrobeats into the mainstream?
8. What event led to riots across England in 2011?
9. How many Black people were living in the UK by the end of the First World War?
10. Which capital cities in Africa have the same names in different languages?
11. What was Nigeria's first capital city?
12. In what year did Choice FM rebrand as Capital Xtra?
13. What was the name of Kano's first album?
14. Who was the first Black model to appear on the cover of *Time* magazine?
15. Who founded Reggae Reggae Sauce?

BLACK HISTORY

ROUND 9

1. Which R&B singer has children with one of Bob Marley's sons?
2. When was the Year of Return?
3. Which Black man was the first person to win *The Apprentice*?
4. Name one of the first six African American musicians to be put in the Rock and Roll Hall of Fame.
5. Kalakuta Republic was formed by which Nigerian artist?
6. Which African country was the last country to gain independence from Britain, and in what year?
7. Which country held the first carnival in the Caribbean?
8. Who made history as the first Black Formula One racing driver?
9. Who was the first Black player to play for Tottenham Hotspur?
10. Which middle-distance runner served in the British Army for nine years?
11. Denise Lewis won gold in the 2000 Olympic Games in which event?
12. In what year was Maggie Alphonsi inducted into the World Rugby Hall of Fame?
13. Who is renowned for being the first hijab-wearing jockey in competitive British horse racing?
14. Who was the first Black British model to enter the *Forbes* models rich list?
15. Who was the first Black woman to become a billionaire?

BLACK HISTORY

ROUND 10

1. Who is the founder of Motown Records?
2. When was Bad Boy Records founded?
3. Which song is the bestselling single by a woman? Both song title and album name are needed.
4. What is the name of the web series that *Insecure* is based on?
5. Who was the first Black woman to win the Academy Award for Best Actress?
6. Who is known as the 'queen of rock and roll'?
7. Who is the first Black filmmaker to win the Academy Award for Best Picture?
8. In what year was the movement Black Lives Matter formed?
9. Who is the world record holder in the men's 100 metres, 200 metres and 4 × 100 metres relay?
10. What is the name of the first Black Disney princess?
11. What was the name of the statutes that forced segregation in the US South in the 19th and early 20th centuries?
12. When is Stephen Lawrence Day?
13. Who was the first hip-hop artist to win the Album of the Year at the Grammys?
14. When was GRM Daily founded?
15. Who was the first Black athlete to compete for Team GB?

BLACK HISTORY

ROUND 11

1. Which Black athlete was inducted into the World Golf Hall of Fame in 2022?
2. Name one of the two co-founders of record label Disturbing London.
3. Who was the first Black woman to win an Emmy for Outstanding Supporting Actress in a Comedy Series?
4. Who is the former CEO of Def Jam records?
5. Which siblings have both had number 1 solo albums?
6. Who was the first African American to be the musical director and conductor of the Academy Awards ceremony?
7. In what year did Zimbabwe gain independence?
8. Who was the first Black professor in the UK?
9. What is the name of the TV show created by Donald Glover?
10. In what year did the Civil Rights Movement start in the US?
11. Who were the co-founders of the Black Panther Party?
12. Which sports star was nicknamed 'The Greatest'?
13. Who was the inventor of the automatic shoe-lasting machine?
14. Who was the first African American in space?
15. What does RAP allegedly stand for?

BLACK HISTORY

ROUND 12

1. Which city is said to be the birthplace of hip-hop?
2. Which cocktail was created by a Ghanaian Brit?
3. Which popular British radio station was previously a pirate radio station?
4. In what year was the film *Cool Runnings* released?
5. Which country was formerly known as French Sudan?
6. What is the name of the president of Burkina Faso who led a coup in 1983?
7. Who is known as the 'queen of soul'?
8. Which Black woman is referred to as the 'mother of rock and roll'?
9. In what year did SB.TV launch?
10. In what year did the Haitian Revolution start?
11. The Haitian Revolution was against which country's colonial rule?
12. Who was the longest-reigning monarch of what is now the Democratic Republic of the Congo?
13. What is the name of the main character of the film *Roots*?
14. Which film based on slavery won nine Academy Award nominations?
15. What TV series included an episode entitled 'Lovers Rock'?

BLACK HISTORY

ROUND 13

1. Which rapper died on 7 September 1996?
2. In what year were the Broadwater Farm riots?
3. What was the first LGBTQ film with an all-Black cast?
4. Who is the founder of the MeToo movement?
5. Which filmmaker was given an Honorary BAFTA Award in 2002?
6. The movie *Think Like a Man* is based on a book written by who?
7. Who is the first Black person to become US vice-president?
8. Who was named artistic director of Louis Vuitton's menswear line in 2018?
9. Which nurse helped to first set up sickle-cell screenings in Britain?
10. Who are the founders of Ruka Hair?
11. Who is the first Black person in the world to earn a master's degree in fashion psychology?
12. Which Black British presenter is the co-host of *Catfish UK*?
13. In what year was Rastafarianism born?
14. Who is the founder of the Nation of Islam?
15. Which British podcast released a *Sunday Times* bestselling book?

BLACK HISTORY

ROUND 14

1. In which country did Robert Mugabe serve as president?
2. Who said the following phrase: 'float like a butterfly, sting like a bee'?
3. Which sub-Saharan African country did Maya Angelou live in?
4. Who was the longest-serving Ghanaian president?
5. What hashtag highlighted police brutality in Nigeria in 2020?
6. In what year was the British Black Panther Movement founded?
7. In what year did the Notting Hill race riots take place?
8. Which author said, 'Your silence will not protect you'?
9. What was Katherine Johnson known for?
10. Who is regarded as Jamaica's first national hero?
11. Who was the first president of the League of Coloured Peoples (LCP)?
12. Who led the boycott of the Bristol Omnibus Company?
13. Who founded the Stephen Lawrence Charitable Trust?
14. Who was the first Black woman to be appointed a Queen's Counsel?
15. What day is Ghana's Independence Day?

BLACK HISTORY

ROUND 15

1. In what year was the Lekki Massacre?
2. Which Black woman became president of the British Science Association in 2021?
3. What was the name of the group of Black activists who led 150 people to march against police harassment of the Black community in Notting Hill?
4. Which Nigerian princess trained as a nurse in London?
5. Who was the leader of the Communist Party USA in the 1960s?
6. Who coined the term 'intersectionality'?
7. Who was the first Black British female book publisher?
8. In what year was the TV channel BET launched?
9. In what year was *Essence* magazine first published?
10. The late 18th Century London-based political group of Black writers were known as 'the____ of Africa'?
11. Where in the US did Rosa Parks refuse to give up her seat?
12. How long did the 1981 Brixton Riots last?
13. What political demonstration followed the New Cross Fire?
14. Who founded *The Voice* magazine?
15. Who was the founder and editor of the *West Indian Gazette*?

BLACK HISTORY

ROUND 16

1. In what year did the Second Congo War start?
2. The statue outside St Thomas' Hospital is of which Black British person?
3. Which Black footballer has a statue outside of Southwark Cathedral?
4. Who said the following: 'Education is the most powerful weapon which you can use to change the world'?
5. Who was the first African American to win the Nobel Peace Prize for Literature?
6. What is the name of the centre in Tottenham named after a Black MP?
7. In what year did Sierra Leone gain independence?
8. Who is the author of *Black Skin, White Masks*?
9. What was the name of the African American who was beaten to death by four police officers in 1991?
10. What song was named 'song of the century' by *Time* magazine in 1999?
11. What was the name of the war that took place in Kenya from 1952 to 1960?
12. Which vocal group sang the song 'Baby Love'?
13. In what year was Bad Boy Records founded?
14. Who said the following: 'When someone shows you who they are, believe them the first time'?
15. *Kaya*, *Uprising* and *Talkin' Blues* are albums by which Black artist?

1980S ROUND

1. Shari Headley, Arsenio Hall and James Earl Jones all starred in which cult classic?
2. In what year was the New Cross Fire?
3. In 1985 Whitney Houston had her first number 1. What was the name of that single?
4. I was voted Sports Personality of the Year in 1982, and won an Olympic gold medal in the decathlon in 1980 and 1984. Who am I?
5. Which political party was in power for the entire decade between 1980 to 1990 in the UK?
6. Which group released the classic anthem 'Rock Steady'?
7. Who was the bestselling artist of the decade?
8. Name the 1986 Act that made it an offence to use threatening, abusive or insulting words or behaviour with intent to stir up racial hatred in the street or in a public speech.
9. Which ceremonial event took place on 29 July 1981?
10. In which country did Desmond Tutu serve as an archbishop?
11. Since 1985, who is the longest-resident character on *EastEnders*?
12. Name the politician elected to Parliament in 1987 who famously attended his first State Opening of Parliament in African dress.
13. Name the group with 'A happy face, a thumpin' bass, for a lovin' race' led by Jazzie B.
14. The Lord's Resistance Army Insurgency is the name for the decades-long upheaval in which country?
15. The song 'All Night Long' released by Lionel Richie appeared on which of his albums?

1990S

ROUND 1

1. What do the initials of American girl group 3LW stand for?
2. According to the character Forrest Gump in the 1994 film, why is life like a box of chocolates?
3. Which Black actor starred in two of the highest-grossing films of the 1990s? Name both actor and the films.
4. 'Do you understand the words that are coming out of my mouth?' is a quote from which film?
5. What are the names of Tommy's parents in *Rugrats*?
6. What was unique about the fight between Mike Tyson and Evander Holyfield?
7. Old Rusty is the name of what in the cartoon series *Recess*?
8. The name of the hip-hop trio Fugees is derived from which word?
9. Hillwood is the name of the home town from which show?
10. What was the name of Chris's best friend in the sitcom *Everybody Hates Chris*?
11. Name the pink character with yellow spots featured on the BBC show *Noel's House Party*.
12. What was the previous name for Starbursts?
13. The Mystery Machine is a van from which show?
14. 'Don't Let Go (Love)' and 'My Lovin' (You're Never Gonna Get It)' were hit singles by which group?
15. What was the name of the ITV show that Cilla Black hosted for 18 years?

1990S

ROUND 2

1. Where did the Million Man March take place?
2. Name the drink brand named after a species of bear that had flavours such as raspberry jelly, ice cream and a limited edition 'Princess Diana Memorial Flavour'.
3. Name the first Black artist to be awarded the Turner Prize for their painting *No Woman, No Cry*.
4. What was the O. J. Simpson trial known as by the US media?
5. Where were the 1996 Olympics held?
6. Name the 1990s R&B girl group consisting of the Higgins sisters, hailing from Manchester.
7. What is the other name for the Belfast Agreement?
8. Who released the song 'Kiss from a Rose'?
9. *The Bodyguard* featured which song by Whitney Houston?
10. Name the toy that can travel down the stairs using the physics phenomena gravity, wave mechanics and momentum.
11. Where did each twin live in the film *The Parent Trap*?
12. What does FUBU stand for?
13. Who released the 1994 hit 'You Gotta Be'?
14. Desert Storm was the name of the US-led liberation of which country that had been invaded by Iraq?
15. What type of person might make you want to have AOL stop your emails or break your lease so you can move?

2000S

ROUND 1

1. What is a G-SHOCK?
2. Fearne Cotton and Reggie Yates hosted which British Sunday-morning children's programme between 2002 and 2004?
3. 'Ha, Ha, Ha! Boom! Boom!' was the contagious laugh from which relaunched TV character?
4. What is the abbreviated term for the year 2000?
5. 'Ping' was a feature used on which device?
6. The cartoon *Watch My Chops* was also known as what?
7. 'Get the London Look' was which brand's slogan?
8. List all the artists on the hit song 'Lean Back'.
9. In what year was LimeWire created?
10. What does SB.TV stand for?
11. How many members form the music group Liberty X?
12. Which pop icon is said to have popularised low-rise jeans in the 2000s?
13. *The Crust, Kerching!* and *50/50* were all shows broadcast on which channel?
14. On the hit show *Friends*, what is the first line of Phoebe's infamous song?
15. What is the name of P Diddy's clothing line?

2000S

ROUND 2

1. To which award show did Justin Timberlake and Britney Spears wear matching denim outfits?
2. Which of the following shows premiered first: *The Suite Life of Zack and Cody, Hannah Montana, Wizards of Waverly Place, That's So Raven*?
3. *The Amanda Show, Are You Afraid of the Dark?* and *The Wild Thornberrys* were all shows screened on which TV channel?
4. 'That's just, like, the rules of feminism' is a quote from which movie?
5. 'Share the luv' was a feature on which old-school social media platform?
6. Which singer wrote the reply to Eamon's 2004 hit, 'F*ck It (I Don't Want You Back)'?
7. On which channel did *Desperate Housewives* air in the UK in 2005?
8. Channel U and Fizz TV were both rebranded to which two channels in 2009?
9. Which launched first, YouTube or Facebook?
10. Dunder Mifflin is a company featured in which sitcom?
11. Finish the following: 'Talk to the ____ cos the face ain't listening'.
12. 'Lose Yourself' by Eminem, 'Love Me' by Eminem, Obie Trice and 50 Cent, and 'Insane in the Brain' by Cypress Hill are all featured on the soundtrack of which film?

13. What was the first Marvel film released in this decade?

14. How many back-to-back shows did Michael Jackson sell out in the O2 Arena in 2009?

15. What was the UK's best-selling novel in the 2000s?

2000S

ROUND 3

1. Which album featured the Kanye classic 'All Falls Down'?
2. Melissa and Arnett are the first names of which hip-hop and R&B 2000s legend?
3. In *Friends*, what two pets do Joey and Chandler own?
4. In the 2000s cult classic *Mean Girls*, according to rules set by the Plastics, on which day of the week were you allowed to wear jeans or track pants?
5. Who wrote the song 'Are You Gonna Bang Doe'?
6. In what TV show did Nicole Richie and Paris Hilton star?
7. What is the name of the country in which simulation game *The Sims* is set?
8. Michelle Williams was brought in to replace which two members of Destiny's Child?
9. Events company and social enterprise Bigga Fish was created in what year?
10. In 2001 EastEnders' famous 'You ain't my mother!' scene came on our screens. After 18 years Kat Slater revealed she was which character's mum?
11. Which boy band trio released the song 'Playground'?
12. 2000s classics 'Last Night', 'Come to Me' and 'I Need a Girl (Part One)' are songs by which artist?
13. In 2007 Tony Blair resigned as prime minister and leader of the Labour Party. Who succeeded him?

14. Name the instant messaging bot that was found on both MSN Messenger and AOL Instant Messenger.

15. What investment bank's declaration of bankruptcy is considered to be the start of the global economic collapse of 2008?

2010S ROUND

1. In what year did Blockbuster close down?
2. In 2013 Choice FM radio station changed its name to what?
3. Name the girl group who released the song 'Black Heart'.
4. In what two years of this decade was same-sex marriage first legalised and then put into effect in the UK?
5. Where did Team GB finish in the medals table in the 2012 Olympics?
6. The Ice Bucket Challenge was originally invented on social media to raise awareness for which disease?
7. Who was prime minister on 1 January 2010?
8. Jordan Stephens and Harley Alexander-Sule formed which musical duo?
9. Which Apple product came out in the first year of this decade?
10. According to the Mayan Calendar, which date in this decade was widely believed to be the day the world would end?
11. For weeks online, there was an ongoing debate as to which two sets of colours a dress were. What were the two-colour-combination options?
12. In 2015, what did Apple allow us to do with our emojis?
13. Name J Hus's 2017 album.
14. Name the series of protests that began in Tunisia at the turn of the decade in response to corruption and economic stagnation.
15. Vine, the precursor to TikTok, was a video-streaming platform that allowed videos of what length to be shared?

7

GEOGRAPHY

These questions are designed to test your general geographical knowledge. Think food, language, travel and beyond. The answers can be found on pages 289–300.

GEOGRAPHY

ROUND 1

1. Kano had it on lock between which two UK cities?
2. One 'After Hours' branch is a few doors down from which London station?
3. Kotoka International Airport is located in which city?
4. Which country has more churches per square kilometre than any other nation in the world?
5. Hackney Peace Carnival Mural is found on which road in London?
6. In UK slang, what does OT mean?
7. Which of the following is *not* a francophone country? Chad, Liberia and Haiti.
8. What are the names of both countries in Asia beginning with J?
9. Vice City and San Andreas are cities in which game?
10. In which Caribbean island is Shirley Heights?
11. How many countries does Togo border?
12. Iouanalao is the former name of which Caribbean island?
13. Kampala is the capital city of which country?
14. Which UK city is referred to as 'The Toon'?
15. Which UK city hosts the largest Diwali festival outside of India?

GEOGRAPHY

ROUND 2

1. Which country is geographically closest to Mauritius?
2. What is the largest country in Africa by area?
3. What country would you be in if you were in the Serengeti?
4. St. John's is the capital city of which country?
5. In which city is the UK's largest exhibition centre?
6. What is the capital of the Bahamas?
7. In what country is *The Boy Who Harnessed the Wind* set?
8. Port of Spain is the capital of which Caribbean country?
9. Name the country completely surrounded by South Africa and that was previously known as Basutoland.
10. In the Caribbean, the ABC Islands are Aruba, Bonaire and what?
11. In the R2Bees song 'Slow Down', where is the sexy girl from?
12. If you were to put all the countries in Europe alphabetical order, which would be first and which would be last?
13. Which country lies between Ghana and Benin?
14. The country previously called Siam is now known as what?
15. Trinity, Blackfriars and Barton Road Swing are all bridges found in which UK city?

GEOGRAPHY

ROUND 3

1. Idris Elba, Lancey Foux and Christine Ohuruogu all hail from which London borough?
2. How many cities are there in the UK?
3. In what year did Sudan and South Sudan separate?
4. What is the largest country in the Caribbean?
5. The Maa language is spoken by which people?
6. A vertical tricolour flag consisting of a blue, gold and red stripe from left to right is which African country's national flag?
7. In Ed Sheeran's song 'Galway Girl', on which street in Dublin did he say he met her?
8. In Stormzy's track 'Still Disappointed', to which country did he claim Wiley's mum had to move?
9. Which Californian city was rapper Roddy Ricch born in?
10. Which boy band released the song 'Mrs. Right', detailing how they would travel all across the world just to meet her?
11. What UK city is Banksy associated with?
12. What is the name of the South African language sometimes referred to as Cape Dutch because of their similarities?
13. Which UK city has become known as the 'city of a thousand trades'?
14. What does UN stand for?
15. How many hemispheres can Africa be found in?

GEOGRAPHY

ROUND 4

1. Which 'W' is the name of the city where Beverley Knight was born?
2. In which country was the film *A Sound of Music* set?
3. The football team Lazio are based in which city?
4. In the Bible, which sea was parted by Moses?
5. Which US state is rapper J. Cole from?
6. Where is the TV show *Waterloo Road* set?
7. The country previously called Upper Volta is now known as what?
8. Merca, Galkayo and Baidoa are cities in which country?
9. An anemometer is used to measure what?
10. Name the closest capital city to the UK.
11. Springfield is home to which animated show?
12. What is the currency in the game *The Sims*?
13. What is the name of the river that runs through London?
14. Comics god Frank Miller said, 'Metropolis is New York City in the daytime; _____ is New York City at night.'
15. In Islam, if you are going on Hajj, which country will you go to?

GEOGRAPHY

ROUND 5

1. What is the official language of Angola?
2. If you were to put all the countries in the Caribbean in alphabetical order, which would be first and which would be last?
3. Which two countries share the world's longest land border?
4. Name the prison in San Francisco Bay.
5. Manama is the capital city of which country?
6. Both Juls and Miriam Makeba released a song featuring the name of which township?
7. In which town was the British comedy *PhoneShop* set?
8. Which country is in both Africa and Asia?
9. What is the second-longest river in the world?
10. Rappers Loyle Carner, Stormzy and Hardy Caprio are from which London borough?
11. What is the only US state with one syllable?
12. Which country was formerly known as Ceylon?
13. Stratus, nimbus and cirrus are all types of what?
14. What are the two US states that are split into North and South?
15. Voice Editor is an anagram for which French-speaking country?

GEOGRAPHY

ROUND 6

1. Put the following continents in order of land-mass size (largest to smallest): Africa, North America, Asia.
2. In which US state was the film *Get Out* shot?
3. In what year did Somalia gain its independence?
4. How many countries are in South America?
5. Finish the title of the song: 'First time in _____' by Naira Marley.
6. In which city is Heriot-Watt University located?
7. What is the name of the estate in *Top Boy*?
8. Santo Domingo is the capital city of which country?
9. Name the luxury shopping outlet near Oxford in the UK.
10. In which city was the first Afro Nation Festival held in 2019?
11. Which US state is home to the most Black people?
12. The Number 1 bus runs from Canada Water to where?
13. Akon, SZA and Chingy are all from which US state?
14. Which station lies between Kennington and Embankment stations on the Northern Line?
15. In which US state is HBCU Morris Brown College?

GEOGRAPHY

ROUND 7

1. In which country is *Love Island*'s winter season filmed?
2. What is the capital of Tunisia?
3. The city of Dire Dawa lies in which country?
4. Which country is the largest exporter of Christmas trees?
5. Where did Adam and Eve live?
6. Bahrain's flag features five white triangles. What do these represent?
7. Name the popular font which is also Latin for the tribes who lived in what is now Switzerland.
8. The Crips gang are originally from which coast of the US?
9. In which country will you find the Volta region?
10. What 'P' is the official language in Aruba and Curaçao?
11. What country are J Hus's parents from?
12. What was the previous name for Eswatini before it changed in 2018?
13. *The Lion, the Witch and the Wardrobe* is set in which fictional location?
14. In which city was the Nigerian singer Aşa born?
15. In 2001, which country was first to legalise same-sex marriage?

GEOGRAPHY

ROUND 8

1. Name the political organisation that was founded in 1931 and as of 2022 had 56 countries as members.
2. Lufthansa is the flag carrier of which country?
3. According to the 2021 census, which borough was the most ethnically diverse in England and Wales?
4. Where did the 2022 football World Cup take place?
5. Name the 2003 Fergie song titled after one of London's landmarks.
6. Guadalajara, Puebla and Acapulco are cities in which country?
7. According to the song 'HYFR', where do all of Drake's exes live?
8. Mount Stanley lies on the border of which two African countries?
9. Which language was the New Testament in the Bible originally written in?
10. Which country is directly north of Chad?
11. Which city is most mentioned in songs?
12. Which country has won the most World Cup football tournaments as of 2022?
13. What does ECOWAS stand for?
14. What is the national animal of the UK?
15. Which London address is the home of the prime minister?

GEOGRAPHY

ROUND 9

1. Which city is rapper Future from?
2. Who wrote the 2011 song 'Rep Your Endz'?
3. The grey crowned crane can be seen at the centre of which country's flag?
4. Name the line that connects Shenfield to Liverpool Street and Abbey Wood to Paddington.
5. Madagascar has the longest coastline in Africa. Which country has the second-longest?
6. What is the name of the UK's largest indoor fish market?
7. In which city is De Montfort University?
8. 'Siete' is the Spanish word for which number?
9. As of 2021, in which location is the franchise *The Real Housewives* based?
10. Name the area in London that was once home to an enormous glass structure built to house the Great Exhibition in 1851, from which it derives its name.
11. Eire is the name of which country in its own language?
12. Portia Simpson-Miller was the prime minister of which country?
13. RG is a postal area in the UK centred on which town?
14. What is the English equivalent of the French name Étienne?
15. A very dry, dusty easterly or north-easterly wind from the Sahara occurring between December and February on the West African coast is known as what?

GEOGRAPHY

ROUND 10

1. Dakar is the capital of which country?
2. Which country's currency code is GHS?
3. How many countries are in North America?
4. The London postal code area IG represents which area of London?
5. In which UK city was the British bakery chain Greggs founded?
6. Which Caribbean nation is known as the Isle of Spice?
7. In which city would you find De Meer Stadion?
8. What is the main export of Burundi?
9. The Māori are the indigenous Polynesian people of which country?
10. Which African country is also a name of a song on Frank Ocean's *Channel Orange* album?
11. How many time zones are there in the continental US?
12. The hit Netflix show *From Scratch* follows Amy Wheeler, an American student who goes to study in which country?
13. Which English city has the third-highest percentage of Black Britons?
14. Arabic is one of the official languages of Algeria. What is the other?
15. Alexandra Palace is in which London borough?

GEOGRAPHY

ROUND 11

1. What is the capital of Haiti?
2. What is the airport code for Lagos Airport?
3. The bestselling novel *The Vanishing Half* follows identical twin sisters Desiree and Estelle 'Stella' Vignes between the 1940s and the 1990s. The twins are light-skinned Black sisters raised in what fictional town?
4. In which country will you typically find a riad?
5. The term 'scouse' is used to denote people from which UK city?
6. Mombassa, Kisumu and Nakuru are all cities of which African country?
7. The Black-owned bookshop New Beacon Books is located in which London borough?
8. Which African country was previously called Dahomey?
9. Jollof rice is said to have originated in which country?
10. How many stations does the London Overground serve?
11. What language is typically spoken in Mauritius?
12. The Black-owned day party Jerk X Jollof was founded in which city?
13. Kano, Akala and Ian Wright all have at least one parent from which Caribbean country?
14. What currency is used in Guadeloupe?
15. Which country in the world ranks second for having the most languages?

GEOGRAPHY

ROUND 12

1. There are two African countries that begin with the letter 'A'. Angola is one; name the other.
2. The Gold Coast was the former name of which country?
3. Which two countries in the Caribbean share an island?
4. In which country can you find the second-highest mountain in Africa?
5. The Mediterranean Sea separates which two continents?
6. Who was 'in San Francisco jamming'?
7. Also known as the Somali Peninsula, what is the most eastern region of Africa called?
8. 'The movement, migration or scattering of a people away from an established or ancestral homeland' is referred to as what?
9. What is the official language of Cape Verde?
10. +251 is the country calling code for which African country?
11. Name the political party in Africa with the largest membership.
12. In which country is the most tequila consumed per person?
13. Widespread electricity blackouts carried out by state-owned energy companies in South Africa are known locally as what?
14. In which city can you find the Promenade des Anglais?
15. *The Fisherman* by Chigozie Obioma is a novel set in which country?

GEOGRAPHY

ROUND 13

1. German South West Africa is the former name of which country?
2. Which mountain in South Africa is also known as Tafelberg?
3. How many country borders does the River Nile run through and along?
4. Castries is the capital city of which Caribbean island?
5. 'An area where there is nothing' is the local name for which desert?
6. Santeria is an Afro-Caribbean religion based on which African belief system and traditions?
7. '5AM in Toronto' is a song by which artist?
8. How many countries in the Caribbean have Spanish as their official language?
9. Quahog is the name of the fictional town that's home to which family?
10. Jamaica's men's team won gold in the 4 × 100 metre relay at the London 2012 Olympics. What leg of the relay did Usain Bolt run?
11. How many four-letter countries are there in Africa?
12. +876 is the country calling code for which Caribbean country?
13. Ghana's Independence Day parade takes place at which landmark?
14. As of 2023, how many Disneylands are there in the world?
15. In which city will you find the Spanish Steps?

GEOGRAPHY

ROUND 14

1. To the nearest hour, how many hours does it take to fly by commercial jet from New York to Los Angeles?
2. In February 2023 Idris Elba announced plans to build a film studio where?
3. What is the capital of Colombia?
4. Which US state is the series *Queen Sugar* set in?
5. What is the largest tribe in Ghana?
6. What country is Diamond Platnumz from?
7. What is the Portuguese acronym for the six Portuguese-speaking African countries?
8. Name the only country in Africa that has Spanish as its official language.
9. In which region of Africa is the Seychelles located?
10. Ga is the traditional abbreviation for which US state?
11. In what area in London can you find the jazz club Troy Bar?
12. In which city is the African Union headquarters located?
13. Rapper Ice Spice revealed she is what two nationalities?
14. So Solid Crew member Swiss has opened a permanent Black Pound Day shop in which UK shopping centre?
15. What is the largest stock exchange in Africa?

GEOGRAPHY

ROUND 15

1. What currency is used in Tunisia?
2. Potomac is a small town in which US state?
3. After you have stopped at Gucci and Louis V, where will Drake fly you out to?
4. Which continent accounts for more than 50 per cent of the world's production of cassava?
5. The four-part BBC TV series *You Don't Know Me* is set in which UK city?
6. Cockburn Town is the capital of which country?
7. What is the country calling code for Sudan?
8. In which UK city is the Marcus Rashford mural?
9. Madesu is a dish made from cannellini beans and a spicy tomato sauce typically found in which country?
10. Bashy, Zadie Smith and Raheem Sterling hail from which part of London?
11. Singer Nimco Happy is from which country?
12. Where in the UK is The Great Escape Festival held?
13. Bamako, Timbuktu and Mopti are all cities in which African country?
14. Caribbean island Aruba's official languages are Papiamento and what?
15. Which New York neighbourhood was referred to as a Black mecca during the 1920s to 1940s?

GEOGRAPHY

ROUND 16

1. Which continent has the most countries?
2. What is Leicester's area code?
3. What is the main religion in Mali?
4. Which flag consists of a black triangle at the hoist, with three horizontal bands of turquoise, gold and turquoise?
5. During which month does the annual Rio Carnival usually take place?
6. Which UK city hosts Europe's oldest West Indian carnival?
7. In January 2023 it was announced that a north London street would be renamed due concerns about its racial connotations. What is the original name of this street?
8. Which international fast-food franchise is said to be a must try when visiting Jamaica?
9. Name the venue where the day-party brand DLT held their first event.
10. What mode of transport do you have to take to get to Freetown, Sierra Leone, from Lungi Airport?
11. Beignets are French deep-fried pastries, usually made from yeast dough. In which US city are they popular?
12. The parents of Daniel Kaluuya, Unknown T and Zawe Ashton all hail from which African country?
13. Name the smallest country in Africa.
14. What is the airport code for Cape Town International Airport?
15. In which US state is Salt Lake City?

GEOGRAPHY

ROUND 17

1. Which country has the second-largest Somali diaspora in Europe?
2. Heron Tower in London is also known as what?
3. What is Jamaican toto?
4. Mustafa the Poet, PartyNextDoor and Winnie Harlow all have which nationality in common?
5. What currency is used in Zambia?
6. The Warehouse Project is a popular series of club nights organised in which UK city?
7. Oxford Street is in which London borough?
8. Wanderlust is a popular indoor/outdoor nightclub in which European city?
9. Swahili originated in East Africa, but how many African countries has the language now spread across?
10. Which Caribbean island is called the 'Rainbow Island'?
11. British actor Adjoa Andoh is from which city?
12. Which county is Wolverhampton in?
13. Colour Factory is a Black-owned nightclub in which London borough?
14. What is the international dialling code for the United Kingdom?
15. What is the acronym for the visa waiver you need to travel from the UK to the US?

GEOGRAPHY

ROUND 18

1. What is the official language of Mozambique?
2. Upton Park tube station is on which two London underground lines?
3. Nicknamed the 'Emerald Isle', what is the smallest state in the Organisation of Eastern Caribbean States (OECS)?
4. Black-owned day-party company Everyday People was founded in which city?
5. In the Netflix series *Money Heist* each gang member is named after a city. Which of the following is not a member of the cast? Stockholm, Lisbon, Vienna and Manila.
6. If you were to put all the US states in alphabetical order, which would be first and which last?
7. I share borders with the following countries: Somalia, Ethiopia, Tanzania and Uganda. What country am I?
8. Which London borough has the largest Black Caribbean population?
9. Which annual celebration takes place in New Orleans the day before Ash Wednesday?
10. Which African country was previously called Zaire?
11. The Waterloo & City line runs between two stations. Name them both.
12. Kizomba is a dance and musical genre that originated in which country?

13. Enish is one of the most popular Nigerian restaurants in London. Which longstanding south London establishment is said to be its rival?

14. Windrush Square is located in which district of London?

15. What is the largest African American music festival that typically takes place annually in Louisiana?

GEOGRAPHY

ROUND 19

1. Tinchy Stryder is from which African country?
2. What is the name of the baked or fried appetiser consisting of pastry and filling that's popular in Latin America?
3. Broadwater Farm, Aylesbury and Heygate are all names of what?
4. On the 'Touch It' remix, which New York borough was on Papoose's middle finger?
5. Quito is the capital of which country?
6. What is located at No. 32 London Bridge Street?
7. The London postal code UB represents which area of London?
8. There are only two countries in the world whose flags contain neither red, white nor blue. Name one of them.
9. According to the 2011 census, which London borough has the highest Black African population?
10. Asmara, Massawa and Mendefera are all cities in which African country?
11. What is the name of the country formerly known as Rhodesia?
12. DXB is the code for which country's international airport?
13. Which London Underground line has the most stations?
14. Which country has the highest Black population outside of Africa?
15. What is the name of the biggest carnival in Barbados, held yearly in August?

GEOGRAPHY

ROUND 20

1. On which London road will you find Bagel King?
2. What is the capital of New Zealand?
3. Which Caribbean island was hit by volcanic eruptions in April 2021?
4. The Black Cultural Archives – London's only national heritage centre dedicated to serving and preserving the history of Afro-Caribbean people – can be found in which district of the city?
5. Ivory Coast is one of the world's top exporters of what?
6. Name the three official languages of Belgium.
7. Which Wood Green to Waterloo TFL bus is also the calling code for the Democratic Republic of the Congo?
8. What is the name of Africa's newest country?
9. In which US state is Barry Jenkins's award-winning film *Moonlight* set?
10. Name the capital of Morocco.
11. Green Park, Stockwell, Warren Street and Walthamstow Central are all stations on which London Underground line?
12. If I wanted to visit the three highest mountains in the world, which continent would I go to?
13. Which African nation has the most pyramids?
14. Lesotho is to which country as Vatican City and San Marino are to Italy?
15. Which city has the second highest Black population in the UK?

GEOGRAPHY

ROUND 21

1. The Democratic Republic of the Congo gained independence from which country in 1960?
2. Which London borough has the highest average house prices?
3. Which country experienced a civil war between the Hutu and the Tutsi ethnic groups?
4. In *Game of Thrones*, Castle Black, Winterfell, the Haunted Forest and the Kingsroad were all filmed in which country?
5. To the nearest billion, how large is the world's population?
6. Harare is the capital city of which country?
7. What is the area code for Liverpool?
8. In which city is the hit TV show *Abbott Elementary* set?
9. Which country announced that they would start the process of removing the British monarch as their head of state in 2022?
10. On what Hackney street is Shelley's salon located in the show *Top Boy*?
11. Name the three countries with only the following three colours in their national flag: red, yellow and black.
12. In the song 'Victory Lap', where did Nipsey Hussle dock at just to smoke?
13. What are the names of the two new tube stations that opened in September 2021 as part of the Northern Line extension?

14. Name the crowded suburb of mainland Lagos, Nigeria, that shares its name with a hit single from Wizkid's second studio album.

15. Which of these is *not* an official London borough? Hillingdon, Blackheath, Redbridge?

GEOGRAPHY

ROUND 22

1. M1llionz, Lotto Boyzz and Mike Skinner all come from which city?
2. Name the capital of Sierra Leone.
3. What country would you be in if you were visiting the Runaway Bay?
4. The Mangrove was a well-known restaurant and meeting spot for activists, authors and musicians in the Black community during the 1960s and 1970s. On which west London road was it located?
5. There are only two landlocked countries in South America. Bolivia is one; name the other.
6. On J. Cole's third studio album *2014 Forest Hills Drive*, track 7 is named after which French town?
7. What is the currency code for Uganda?
8. Wembley can be found in which London borough?
9. If you were to put all the countries in Africa in alphabetical order, which would be first and which would be last?
10. Name any two countries forming part of the Maghreb.
11. What is the most westerly point in mainland England?
12. What bus number does Dave reference in his track 'Streatham'?
13. Which country is said to have the most languages in the world?
14. Which of the following is *not* a stop on the Central Line? Park Royal, Stratford, Shepherd's Bush.
15. What city was the intended destination of the *Titanic* in its maiden voyage in 1912?

GEOGRAPHY

ROUND 23

1. Rodney Bay is in which Caribbean island?
2. Where was the first Morley's shop opened?
3. What is the largest state in the US?
4. Skepta, Chip and Adele come from which London borough?
5. In which area of London is the Addey & Stanhope School?
6. 21 Savage and Ghetts come from which London borough?
7. If your water broke while you were in the Prince of Peckham, what is the nearest hospital?
8. In which modern-day country was Saint Nicholas (Father Christmas) born?
9. What are the two official languages of Kenya?
10. Method Man, Ja Rule and Jadakiss were all born in which US state?
11. As a part of regeneration/gentrification plans, Elephant & Castle is being rebranded under what name?
12. If you and your mates wanted to eat a delicious Turkish mixed-grill platter for dinner, where out of north, east, south or west London would be the best place to go?
13. Name the south London district, where, according to the Harlem Spartans, 'it started'.
14. If all the countries in the world were listed in alphabetical order, which country would appear first?
15. What colour is the Elizabeth Line?

GEOGRAPHY

ROUND 24

1. In which continent is the Republic of Suriname?
2. What is the smallest borough in London by area?
3. If you are from Saint Vincent, what is your nationality?
4. What is the national currency of Eritrea?
5. Cairo is the most populous city in Africa. Name the second-most populous.
6. What is the nationality of someone born in Dubai?
7. A blue background with 12 five-pointed gold stars arranged in a circle in the centre is a description of which flag?
8. In which European country can you find the largest African diaspora?
9. In 2022, videos of Extinction Rebellion protestors being dragged off tube trains by commuters went viral. At which station did this incident take place?
10. The prime minister of Ethiopia won the 2019 Nobel Peace Prize for negotiating peace with which country?
11. Where was McDonald's first ever branch in London?
12. What is the capital of Barbados?
13. Which London Underground station has the most London Underground lines?
14. The festival formerly known as the Caribana Carnival takes place in which city?
15. In WSTRN's track 'Ben' Ova', where does Haile say he has come from?

8

POLITICS

This round covers both British and world politics –
enjoy! The answers can be found on page 301.

POLITICS ROUND

1. The JLP and the PNP are the two main political parties of which country?
2. On which day of the week are Prime Minister's Questions (PMQs) held?
3. Which prime minister confessed in a 2017 interview that the naughtiest thing they had done was run through a field of wheat?
4. Who was appointed Secretary of State for International Development in 2003 and became the first Black woman to be elected to cabinet?
5. How many years did Nelson Mandela spend in prison?
6. When did the UK referendum on membership of the EU take place? Month and year needed.
7. Which 'B' describes MPs or members of the House of Lords that are neither government ministers nor opposition Shadow spokespeople.
8. Sir Lindsay Hoyle, John Bercow and Michael Martin have all held which position in UK politics?
9. Who said, 'The white man's happiness cannot be purchased by the black man's misery'?
10. Who was the first African American woman to be elected to the US Congress?
11. Kwasi Kwarteng was elected MP for which constituency?
12. In his incomprehensible viral statement Patrick Obahiagbon said Nigeria still wallows in a state of ethnocentric what?

13. Name any one of the founders of the British Black Panther Movement.
14. What was the subject of the UK referendum held in 2011?
15. What is the name of the UK's leading independent race equality think tank?

9

FOOD AND DRINK

If food is the way to your heart, then this round should be a walk in the park as here we are putting your food-and-drink knowledge to the test. The answers can be found on pages 301–303.

FOOD AND DRINK

ROUND 1

1. What is a cornicione on a pizza?
2. What is the national dish of Egypt, consisting of rice, lentils, pasta and chickpeas?
3. An alcoholic beverage that you would like served with ice is described as what?
4. What are people who work at Nando's known as?
5. A UK-based rap duo opened a dessert restaurant in Croydon under what name?
6. What is the name for foods that are approved for consumption by Jews?
7. Which high-end bakery has been widely accepted as a signal of an area being gentrified?
8. What gives the dish Ayamase its distinct green colour?
9. What does GMO stand for?
10. What gives the condiment Marmite its unique flavour?
11. 'Twist, lick and dunk' are instructions for eating which popular snack?
12. What is a stinking bishop?
13. In what year was a sugar tax introduced in the UK?
14. What is the Spanish word for chicken?
15. What is the name for a style of video content where creators eat while talking to their audience online?

FOOD AND DRINK

ROUND 2

1. Tostones, mofongo and pastelon are all made with which fruit?
2. Tahini is made from ground what?
3. In cockney rhyming slang, 'Bread and _____' means money?
4. The cocktail known as sex on the beach is made with which two spirits?
5. What is the Arabic word for 'permissible'?
6. The Nigerian dish asaro is also known as what?
7. What is the name for the mild and sweet BBQ dressing offered on the Nando's menu?
8. Name the spice that has anti-inflammatory properties, stains bright orange and is in the ginger family.
9. UK supermarket Sainsbury's changed their slogan to 'Helping everyone eat better'. What was it previously?
10. Name the award given to restaurants for their outstanding cooking, ingredients and flavours.
11. Nigerian agege bread is referred to as what in the Caribbean?
12. 'Little fried and golden thing' is the translation for which brand of snack?
13. What is the name of the Nickelodeon character obsessed with orange soda?
14. Name the Indian restaurant in *EastEnders* run by the Masood family.
15. Red wine traditionally pairs well with what in fine dining?

FOOD AND DRINK

ROUND 3

1. In which European country are 12 grapes traditionally eaten at midnight on New Year's Eve?
2. In November 2022 it was announced that which chocolate was to be removed from some tubs of Celebrations?
3. What is the main ingredient in Kenyan matoke?
4. Jamaican bammy is a type of what?
5. What colour is the flesh of the fruit guava?
6. What type of food is gazpacho?
7. Which country is widely accepted to be where coffee originated?
8. Finish the saying 'I love you like _____ food.'
9. Name the Louisiana dish consisting of meat, seafood, vegetables and rice.
10. On which London street was the first 805 opened?
11. Muslims typically break their fast with which fruit?
12. What is the name for a person who eats fish but not meat.
13. What makes a pornstar martini different from a regular martini?
14. Which type of tequila has aged longer, anejo or reposado?
15. What is the main ingredient in the Jamaican dish rundown?

FOOD AND DRINK

ROUND 4

1. Name the cocktail that consists of white rum, lime juice and simple syrup.
2. Which country is the leading exporter of coffee?
3. What is the name of the Black-owned shop based in East London specialising in chocolate?
4. What is the main ingredient used to make hummus?
5. Shishito, Aleppo and ata rodo are all types of what?
6. Which ingredient gives Jamaican patties their flaky texture?
7. What is the Ghanaian name for the snack Nigerians refer to as puff-puff?
8. Name the 24-hour eatery on the Walworth Road named after its speciality.
9. Which country is considered the birthplace of rum?
10. The Mangrove was a historical Black British restaurant located in which area of London?
11. The traditional Ghanaian dish kenkey is made from grains of what?
12. What is gizzada?
13. Who is the owner of the Islington restaurant 12:51?
14. Electric Avenue outdoor market is located in which district of London?
15. Thieboudienne is the national dish of which country?

10

EVENTS

This one is for the outside crew, so expect questions on your favourite carnivals, festivals and nights out. The answers can be found on page 303.

EVENTS ROUND

1. The Rio Carnival is traditionally meant to celebrate the start of what?
2. 'Enjoy your life' is the motto for which of London's favourite event nights?
3. In what year did Jay-Z, Rihanna, Justin Timberlake and Kendrick Lamar all perform at the Wireless Festival?
4. Strawberries & Creem Festival takes place in which UK city?
5. The event FOL, held by the Redeemed Christian Church of God, stands for what?
6. The Guap Gala took place for the first time in 2022 in which iconic location?
7. What do the initials of Black British-owned day-party brand DLT stand for?
8. Name the annual outdoor festival in London that is the largest celebration for Ghanaians in the diaspora.
9. Speakers' Corner, the Serpentine and the Bavarian Village are all located in which annual venue?
10. Beyoncé announced her 2011 pregnancy with a belly rub at which award show?
11. In which UK city were the MOBOs held in 2021?
12. Name the festival organised by Stormzy in Ibiza.
13. Annual event Afrochella changed its name to what in 2022?
14. Pyramid, West Holts and John Peel are stages at which major music festival?
15. Attendees consume 240,000 hand-crafted tea-cakes, 80,000 cups of tea and 56,000 bottles of champagne at which prestigious five-day annual sporting event?

11

MERRY QUIZMAS!

One of our favourite times of the year! This round is all things Christmas. The answers can be found on page 304.

MERRY QUIZMAS! ROUND

1. Hibiscus flower petals, ginger, allspice and orange peel are just some of the ingredients in which Jamaican festive drink?

2. Which UK company's Christmas advert is the UK official favourite?

3. I am a popular baked side dish in the Black community. You will find me on many festive menus and in university halls. What am I?

4. In the holiday classic *The Best Man Holiday*, the men of the group sing which song during the talent-show scene?

5. What is the term used for the street parades that typically take place on many islands across the Caribbean on both Boxing Day and New Year's Day?

6. Patti LaBelle, Jennifer Hudson and Mariah Carey have all recorded versions of which Christmas classic?

7. In which two gospels will you be able to find the Nativity story?

8. In the Christmas classic by Destiny's Child, on the eighth day of Christmas they got a pair of Chloé shades *and* a what?

9. Name the celebrity stylist and influencer loved for their annual Advent calendar daily reviews.

10. What was the widely watched Netflix movie of 2018 on Christmas Day?

11. Name the celebration observed by African Americans from 26 December to 1 January.

12. Which actor made their directorial debut with the 2021 Christmas film *Boxing Day*?

13. Who was the last Black person to have a UK Christmas number 1? Both song title and artist are needed.
14. Every year the diaspora fly out to Ghana and Nigeria for the festive party season. What is this period known as?
15. Rapper DMX is associated with which Christmas song after he freestyled it on Power 105.1 Radio?

12

PUZZLES

This next section is for the visual learners. We have a collection of puzzle-style games that will test your knowledge across a range of categories. The answers can be found on pages 304–313.

ANAGRAMS – ICONIC BLACK AND MIXED BRITISH FOOTBALLERS ROUND

1. Wraithing
2. Cords Musharraf
3. Dorian Finder
4. Bello Clamps
5. Blacken Wendy
6. Cleo Halsey
7. Cods Johanna
8. Healing Jumbled
9. Emylee Hikes
10. Wot Teacloth
11. Defame Joiner
12. Jam Advised
13. Asher Remelting
14. Alice Pun
15. Athene Kiddie

ANAGRAMS – 90S US RAPPERS ROUND

1. The Equal Fina
2. At CPU
3. Ahmed Mont
4. App Planets
5. Bice Cue
6. Booing Suitor
7. My Celt
8. BC Talk Though
9. Il Milk
10. Seam
11. Hilary Null
12. Boxy for NW
13. Good Pongs
14. Tiles Moistly
15. Elite Safely

ANAGRAMS – CLASSIC GARAGE AND FUNKY SONGS ROUND

1. 'Abey Backs'
2. 'Alcott Echo Weeklies'
3. 'Block Tillie Tufta'
4. '21 CD Noses'
5. 'Another Kerb'
6. 'Darth Pray'
7. 'Karim Sneaking'
8. 'Hosted Overflowing'
9. 'Minny Mod'
10. 'Toft Vamoosin'
11. 'Hermon Tining'
12. 'Genie Slurp'
13. 'Latin Melt'
14. 'Demon Goo 4'
15. 'Che True & Shea Cute'

ANAGRAMS – GRIME ARTISTS ROUND

1. Ask Pet
2. Akon
3. Mad Nevil
4. Roz Myst
5. Asherr Dully
6. Cater Jay
7. IV Stolen
8. Dr L Flat
9. A Lyon
10. Deck II
11. Eli Sons
12. My Open
13. Bleed Duo
14. Hi PC
15. Fifi Salaam

ANAGRAMS – BLACK BRITISH FILMS ROUND

1. *Firm Nag*
2. *Any Blob*
3. *Navaho Duo*
4. *Bob Tulley*
5. *KC Ros*
6. *Ask Nh*
7. *Tenth Tine*
8. *Adi Rey*
9. *Abbot Rhyme*
10. *Bottle Hack Tack*
11. *Gaby Dixon*
12. *A Priest*
13. *Berty Soul*
14. *Ethel Treats*
15. *Kohl Outdid*

ANAGRAMS – BLACK CARTOON CHARACTERS ROUND

1. Ameline Ferry
2. Pony Pruned
3. Archie Musicales
4. Acorn Newel Blvd
5. Collar Scran
6. Mr Sot
7. Arc Terret XII
8. Irrelevance Panellist
9. Joshes Rangeland
10. Bum Five Hun
11. KC Rob
12. Moe Quin
13. Deer Jargon
14. Aloe Slimmers
15. My Sis

ANAGRAMS – REALITY TV ROUND

1. *Bob Righter*
2. *Avon Held Hippo*
3. *Maimed Redirection*
4. *Abba Silk Twelves*
5. *Bald Big Curls*
6. *Bled Violins*
7. *Euros Huns*
8. *Olav Off Velor*
9. *Dural Argues Crap*
10. *Gratified Rams Thirst*
11. *Atlantis Piedmont*
12. *Elfie West*
13. *Femes Inks Patch*
14. *Benjie Escalators*
15. *Astronomical Exempted*

ANAGRAMS – FOOD AND DRINK (DIASPORA FAVOURITES) ROUND

1. Gam mun
2. Crawfish poundings
3. TB roof
4. Ached menaces
5. Frolic Joel
6. Mules part
7. Tariffless thirst
8. A wry & hew pen
9. Anon raftage
10. Fabe petty
11. Jink recheck
12. Alan pint
13. Alfie's TV
14. Awl close
15. Ai tempe

ANAGRAMS – BLACK TV SHOWS ROUND

1. *Boston Choked*
2. *The Foul Pyramid*
3. *Knifed Midways*
4. *Saul Fol*
5. *Shab Lick*
6. *Nice Ruse*
7. *Filers Grind*
8. *Resist Resits*
9. *Adore Very Shy Bitches*
10. *Ankle & Knee*
11. *Lans Wolf*
12. *Benjamin Garey*
13. *Chug Mewing*
14. *Is Cher*
15. *Feel Range*

ANAGRAMS – THROWBACK BRANDS ROUND

1. Addy Her
2. PR Stay
3. Allin Frank Marshland
4. Glue Interior
5. Cut Juice Your
6. Xavier
7. Awe Ren
8. Pah Tabby
9. Auto Lubes Quip
10. Donah Theorist
11. Harrell Puna
12. IV Use
13. Conch Ttys
14. Gas RT
15. Masque Tara

ANAGRAMS – LATE-20TH-CENTURY TECH ROUND

1. Berkly Crab
2. Dippy Folks
3. Atomic Ghat
4. Lank Maw
5. Bogy Mae
6. Roper Joct
7. Arin Ferd
8. Arvy Helps
9. Ail Dup
10. Cami Flamer
11. Pearly 3PM
12. A Niko
13. Don Piano
14. Don Intends
15. Felon Phip

FILL IN THE BLANKS

1. New Age simile/descriptor _ _ _ / G _ _ _ _ _
2. Understood _ A _ / _ _ _ _
3. Person, thing, item, girl _ _ W _
4. Nothing you can do, so . . . _ _ _ R _ _/ _ _
5. Hit the trap and get it back _ _ _ _ / AN / _
6. How Maya Jama family-zoned Margs _ _ _ _ _ _ _ _ _ _
7. No stress, no wahala – everything easy _ O _ _/ _ _ F _
8. Under duress (TikTok reference) T _ _/ _ _ _ _ _ _ _ _ _/ IS/ _ _ _ _ _ _ _/ W _ _ _ _ _
9. The state of the dating scene _ _ _ _ _ _ _ _/ _ R _/ _ O _ D
10. Hitting the lottery/God coming through _ _ N _/ _ _ _ _ _ _
11. A madness _ _ _ _ _ A
12. Disappearing on a potential _ _ _ _ _ _ D
13. To hit/insult – unpleasant looking _ L _ _ _ _ D
14. Bagged red-handed _ _ U _ _ _/ _ N/ _ _
15. Phrase, zero lies told _ O/ _ A _

BLACK THEATRE WORD SEARCH

Dreamgirls	Red Pitch	Hamilton
Get Up, Stand Up	Small Island	For Black Boys
Sister Act	Three Sisters	The Fisherman
Barber Shop Chronicles	The Lion King	Sylvia
Misty	A Number	House of Life

```
O P N Q R K H I F D J I E H R L L R P R
B A R B E R S H O P C H R O N I C L E S
U M E Y H Q P F Z Q N D B X N I G N V D
T R G V B N Y D D H B F F X D B F G F H
H A S E V O I F V R S Y L V I A N V U O
R T V I T B O I P D E W T X Q D Y J G U
E J H K S U G P T S G D O Y P O D Y P S
E A D E E T P L H S D D P X O C U C C E
S I K O F R E S C A J S V I N A J U V O
I D J A E I W R T R M I X O T Z P W O F
S C Y M N A S E A A S I P H E C Z A K L
T H G I U U G H T C N F L U L I H D Y I
E T T S W K M M E L T D W T H F Z R P F
R G P T F O H B I R C G U X O V F E L E
S Q U Y X P G P E R M T N P P N R A N A
X T Y E I H X X Y R L A W W W P X M F J
I I A G N Q E N D S S L T Y H H H G V T
S M A L L I S L A N D S N B G M J I H N
X K W M F O R B L A C K B O Y S G R K U
X U T H E L I O N K I N G R N Y Z L P B
```

POPULAR DANCES WORD SEARCH

Superman	Stanky Legg	Cutting shapes
Coupé-décalé	Ndombolo	Dougie
Shaku	Nae Nae	Rumba
Twerk	Migraine skank	Azonto
Odi	Crip walk	Candy

```
C R S X G H L U O C K N D O M B O L O K
Z O S B O X E U R J E Z Y S H A K U I M
M R U F R G C B G L G Q B I P E D N G A
L A F P F A C Q I J Z P C O H T O B A V
L Z X L É O E U A R J Z K D W P U T Z C
Q O L M K D D I T F E H V I T P G N N N
M N X F C S É F Q T W Y P F H B I X A Q
P T M Q Q N F C R J I W G E C H E D E J
H O I C A N D Y A Z H N C V U K P F N L
D T G V G S P P O L P K G F K V A M A V
T U R S F Q T O T A É Y H S E C X A E I
P M A N U J E A X W P K X V H L P S M W
A C I F L P X M N P E P A B U A Q X Q L
X R N I F S E I D K A R Y T F V P G J G
J I E Z D N Y R D V Y A K V S J C E W W
J P S S V M A J M A O L E N G F Z W S S
Z W K E G S O Y K A S R E J V G M E O S
V A A H O R U M B A N T S G N T L A Y J
L L N H J X G I N I A A R G G W A N U M
R K K G T N V Z E X A J U I F V P X U Q
```

TV AND FILM WORD SEARCH

Get Out	Half of a Yellow Sun	Kerching!
Think Like a Man	City of Gods	The Wedding Party
Girls Trip	Coming to America	Rush Hour
Hidden Figures	Hitch	Rocks
Paid in Full	Sister Act	Fruitvale Station

```
H  W  P  A  I  D  I  N  F  U  L  L  D  K  G  N  Q  W  H  S
L  N  G  I  R  L  S  T  R  I  P  E  I  U  K  G  F  C  G  V
F  R  U  I  T  V  A  L  E  S  T  A  T  I  O  N  A  O  E  E
B  H  I  D  D  E  N  F  I  G  U  R  E  S  V  I  M  M  Y  S
V  X  V  H  Q  M  N  I  E  C  P  H  V  J  M  X  Y  I  H  P
B  H  M  T  A  T  H  I  N  K  L  I  K  E  A  M  A  N  H  W
L  E  U  J  L  L  H  M  M  X  O  E  C  N  T  W  D  G  E  A
T  B  C  A  E  L  F  E  G  T  L  J  K  X  D  R  J  T  S  V
D  W  V  I  E  J  C  O  W  M  E  Z  N  V  R  N  I  O  D  A
B  T  H  I  T  C  H  X  F  E  W  U  Q  C  O  I  J  A  I  D
H  S  R  D  W  Y  U  W  Q  A  D  B  W  R  C  E  Q  M  T  L
K  G  I  G  X  E  O  K  H  U  Y  D  X  E  K  R  C  E  J  R
E  J  R  S  E  L  D  F  Z  O  A  E  I  W  S  D  C  R  I  O
R  P  U  U  T  T  C  W  G  M  B  U  L  N  R  X  D  I  A  S
C  D  V  L  S  E  O  U  T  O  I  P  B  L  G  Q  K  C  R  I
H  C  Q  L  B  H  R  U  L  U  D  I  M  Z  O  P  P  A  Z  E
I  Y  C  I  L  B  H  A  T  K  R  S  B  F  L  W  A  T  R  N
N  Q  C  W  D  J  N  O  C  D  B  N  Z  S  E  P  S  R  O  J
G  S  L  O  G  X  A  L  U  T  X  K  U  U  V  L  E  U  T  T
H  W  Q  M  W  U  G  I  Z  R  Y  R  A  G  F  B  Q  Y  N  Y
```

MAP OF THE WORLD

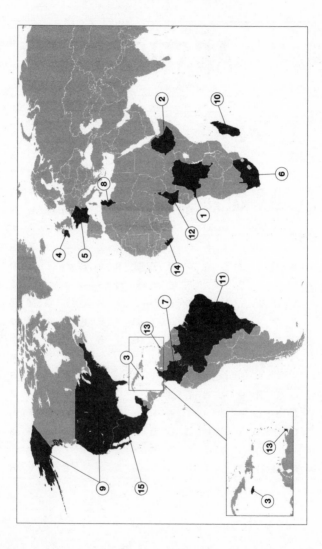

Name the 15 countries shown on the map

ANSWERS

NOT-SO-GENERAL KNOWLEDGE

ROUND 1

1. Calendly
2. Spider
3. Ultra-Low Emission Zone
4. Gboyega Odubanjo
5. Straight flush
6. Wretch 32
7. Green
8. Lisa Maffia
9. 22 June
10. Modie
11. Missy Elliott
12. Pain
13. Naomi Campbell
14. Ade
15. Brixton

NOT-SO-GENERAL KNOWLEDGE

ROUND 2

1. Eid
2. *Arthur*
3. Wahala
4. Lenny Henry
5. 1987
6. Dr Kananga
7. Bahamian dollar
8. Burna Boy
9. Diane Abbott
10. Only the family
11. Easter
12. Vegetable
13. Gari
14. Stormzy
15. Viola Davis

NOT-SO-GENERAL KNOWLEDGE

ROUND 3

1. Eggplant
2. Claudia Jones
3. Kemi Badenoch
4. 1967
5. Tagine
6. Big Brovaz
7. Sierra
8. Aging
9. K Koke
10. Brent
11. Foot
12. Sunni Islam
13. Advancement
14. Denise Fox
15. Plantain

NOT-SO-GENERAL KNOWLEDGE

ROUND 4

1. Gabon
2. Arsenal and Tottenham
3. Washington, DC
4. Moses
5. Ethiopia
6. Wizkid
7. Baby Guinness
8. Shona
9. Asia
10. Red blood cells
11. Lettuce
12. Church of England bishop
13. Halle Bailey
14. Ghana
15. Faridah Àbíké-Íyímídé

NOT-SO-GENERAL KNOWLEDGE

ROUND 5

1. Hispaniola
2. *Mama Goes to Market*
3. October
4. Belgrave Square
5. Reggie Yates
6. North Africa
7. Issa Rae
8. Newham
9. 2011
10. Gele
11. John Boyega
12. Ridley Road Market
13. In his drop-top cruising the streets
14. Ackee and saltfish
15. Destiny's Child

NOT-SO-GENERAL KNOWLEDGE

ROUND 6

1. Section Boyz
2. Mammals
3. Michaela Coel
4. Nigeria
5. Mis-Teeq
6. Indonesia
7. Using their hands/ gestures to articulate their point
8. Portugal
9. Ealing/Earl's Court
10. 2007
11. Birmingham to Amsterdam
12. Talia Hibbert
13. Sugababes
14. Left hand
15. Yinka Shonibare

NOT-SO-GENERAL KNOWLEDGE

ROUND 7

1. 'Father, into thy hands I commend my spirit'
2. Femi Oyeniran
3. Birmingham
4. Jae5
5. Kiss FM
6. Skunk Anansie
7. Shy FX
8. Lizzie Damilola Blackburn
9. Ghana
10. David Olusoga
11. Carat
12. Steven Bartlett
13. Angellica Bell
14. Armed robbery
15. Reni Eddo-Lodge

NOT-SO-GENERAL KNOWLEDGE

ROUND 8

1. Best New Artist
2. 1970s
3. Brent South
4. 22
5. FLO
6. Regina King
7. Jordan Dunne
8. 2010
9. *The Wire*
10. Mantle
11. Marvin Sapp
12. Wives'
13. Twins
14. Congo (now Democratic Republic of the Congo)
15. Sir Alexander Bustamante

NOT-SO-GENERAL KNOWLEDGE

ROUND 9

1. TikTok
2. Tinie Tempah
3. Eddie Kadi
4. Pimples
5. Yellow and blue
6. Juici Jerk
7. Harrods
8. Germany
9. LAPP the Brand
10. Jacky Wright
11. 1991
12. D&G
13. Taller Than Your Average
14. Sounds
15. His Majesty's Revenue and Customs

NOT-SO-GENERAL KNOWLEDGE

ROUND 10

1. Bush
2. Lemar
3. Black, Indigenous (and) People of Colour
4. Igbo
5. *Americanah*
6. Trevor Noah
7. Nia Long
8. Reggie Yates
9. Bolivia
10. Bait
11. 1999
12. It can be tumble-dried
13. Mount Kilimanjaro
14. Fyre Festival
15. Cheese

NOT-SO-GENERAL KNOWLEDGE

ROUND 11

1. Las Olas
2. Bree Runway
3. Westminster Abbey
4. Dizzee Rascal
5. Jake
6. So Solid Crew
7. Meerkat
8. *The Order of the Phoenix*
9. 1945
10. LaGuardia
11. 2007
12. Caleb Azumah Nelson
13. Dwarf
14. Jeremiah 29:11
15. Herd

NOT-SO-GENERAL KNOWLEDGE

ROUND 12

1. Hinduism
2. Graphics Interchange Format
3. SCUBA diving
4. Danish
5. Shirley Ambrose
6. Season 2
7. Del Boy and Rodney
8. *Captain Phillips*
9. Sam's Chicken
10. *Angus, Thongs and Full-Frontal Snogging*
11. Tony Blair
12. John Major
13. 2002
14. Tyler Perry
15. Bashy

NOT-SO-GENERAL KNOWLEDGE

ROUND 13

1. Rolex watch
2. South Sudan
3. 'Body' by Tion Wayne and Russ Millions
4. St Kitts and Nevis
5. Aaron and Stefan
6. Spider
7. Axel Blake
8. Screwball
9. Abraham
10. Seven
11. 'Stand by Me'
12. Guy Fawkes
13. Coding languages
14. Salem Saberhagen
15. Apu

NOT-SO-GENERAL KNOWLEDGE

ROUND 14

1. Kensington & Chelsea
2. 15 years
3. Lionel Messi
4. *You Don't Know Me*
5. November 2020
6. 2017
7. Basenji
8. Bird
9. Bahamas
10. Michaela Coel
11. Króna
12. Adam's apple
13. South Africa
14. Zambia
15. Artist

NOT-SO-GENERAL KNOWLEDGE

ROUND 15

1. *Love Island*
2. Olive
3. France
4. Science, Technology, Engineering and Mathematics
5. 'Sure Thing'
6. Black British beauty and hair shops
7. They lose their go
8. Paul and Barry
9. The papacy
10. Beta Squad
11. Cat Burns
12. Double jeopardy
13. Benjart
14. Lashana Lynch
15. National Basketball Association

NOT-SO-GENERAL KNOWLEDGE

ROUND 16

1. 10v10
2. Samuel L. Jackson
3. Patience Ozokwor
4. Eat Out to Help Out
5. Canaan
6. John Boyega
7. Canary Wharf
8. International Design
9. Busta Rhymes
10. *Renaissance* by Beyoncé
11. Keith David
12. Rice
13. Quarter Quell
14. 'Don't Rush' challenge
15. Eartha Kitt

NOT-SO-GENERAL KNOWLEDGE

ROUND 17

1. 2002
2. Technology, Entertainment, Design
3. A sausage
4. Purple
5. Soprano, alto, tenor and bass
6. M1llionz
7. The Obamas
8. Jiggle jiggle
9. Maryland
10. Red
11. *World's Strictest Parents*
12. Insult
13. Dami 'Oloni' Olonisakin
14. Don Jazzy
15. Chief Nana Bonsu

NOT-SO-GENERAL KNOWLEDGE

ROUND 18

1. Jackets
2. Beverly
3. Skip a go
4. Adkins
5. St Francis Xavier
6. Aries
7. Eternal
8. Tequila
9. Biff, Chip and Kipper
10. Walter Rodney
11. An OBE
12. Doctor Who
13. Moira Stewart
14. Diss tracks
15. Nala's Baby

NOT-SO-GENERAL KNOWLEDGE

ROUND 19

1. *Vogue*
2. KSI
3. 1997
4. Joseph
5. Win an Olympic gold medal
6. Gospel
7. Prophet Musa (PBUH)
8. The ballpoint pen
9. BlackBerry phone
10. Jennifer Lopez in her green Versace dress
11. Brenda Fassie
12. Scar
13. Necessity
14. Supermalt
15. The Ten Commandments

NOT-SO-GENERAL KNOWLEDGE

ROUND 20

1. Moscato
2. 14
3. Eric Effiong in *Sex Education*
4. White Garment
5. 90s Baby Show
6. Iain Sterling
7. Nintendo 64, Game Boy Color, Game Boy Advance, GameCube, Nintendo DS
8. Identity code
9. 2015
10. *Sometimes I Might Be Introvert*
11. 50 ml
12. National Youth Day
13. Fela Kuti
14. Cat
15. James Bond

NOT-SO-GENERAL KNOWLEDGE

ROUND 21

1. Malt beer and fruit
2. 30 days
3. Cassava leaves
4. Alice Walker
5. Black British-owned clothing brands
6. Hiram Revels
7. Shawarma
8. If Allah wills it/God willing
9. TV licence fee
10. Black Panther
11. Octagon
12. Spinach
13. Any other business
14. South Africa
15. Diane Abbott

NOT-SO-GENERAL KNOWLEDGE

ROUND 22

1. Silk press
2. 12
3. Biscuit
4. 'Every little helps'
5. 8
6. Margarita
7. Muhammad
8. Maya Angelou
9. Extra mild
10. The Daniel Fast
11. Breakfast
12. Libya
13. 'Teach Me How to Dougie'
14. Stew
15. Shift, Command and 3

NOT-SO-GENERAL KNOWLEDGE

ROUND 23

1. Very good looking
2. Banksy
3. Squid
4. 'I wanna be a baller'
5. Republic of Biafra
6. Sudoku
7. Dance
8. Bat mitzvah
9. 'I've been deeping, I've been deeping, I've been deeping it.'
10. Taurus, Virgo and Capricorn
11. Yaa Gyasi
12. Magnavox Odyssey
13. Chickpeas
14. Akelle Charles, Haile and Louis Rei
15. Ibeji

NOT-SO-GENERAL KNOWLEDGE

ROUND 24

1. Residential flats
2. Billy Porter
3. Corn and rice
4. 'Striking Vipers'
5. Hair/grease
6. Fajr
7. Tej
8. Salahe Bembury
9. 16
10. Snail mucin
11. Two
12. Christian denominations
13. JT and Yung Miami
14. Yorkshire pudding
15. Xscape

NOT-SO-GENERAL KNOWLEDGE

ROUND 25

1. Snap
2. 2017
3. Caterpillar
4. Red kidney beans
5. Shia
6. Tramway Path
7. 'To Zion'
8. Daps
9. Bahamas
10. Brent Central
11. Mormonism
12. Whoopi Goldberg and Jennifer Hudson
13. National Electric Power Authority
14. 40 years
15. Frame reformer

NOT-SO-GENERAL KNOWLEDGE

ROUND 26

1. Before anything else
2. Orange and T-Mobile
3. Simp
4. *Ordinary People*
5. High-intensity interval training
6. Young Adz
7. Ethiopia
8. Swallow
9. Andrea Levy
10. Steak
11. August
12. Bismillah
13. Green tea leaves
14. Chrissy Teigen
15. Card game

NOT-SO-GENERAL KNOWLEDGE

ROUND 27

1. Safeway
2. Fergie, will.i.am, apl.de.ap and Taboo
3. *There's Mo to Life*
4. Ace of Spades
5. Converse
6. Tania Nwachukwu
7. Excel
8. Spain
9. True
10. Grenadine
11. Mariah Carey/$E=MC^2$
12. Seventh-day Adventists
13. Soho House
14. Acidic
15. 3c

NOT-SO-GENERAL KNOWLEDGE

ROUND 28

1. Guinness punch
2. *Things Fall Apart*
3. To end
4. East
5. Fantasy Football
6. Deborah Meaden, Peter Jones, Sara Davies, Touker Suleyman and Steven Bartlett
7. Afro-house
8. Lewisham East
9. Burberry
10. True
11. Presenter
12. Kelly Clarkson
13. Lori and Steve Harvey
14. Apple
15. 6

NOT-SO-GENERAL KNOWLEDGE

ROUND 29

1. Music-streaming platform
2. A 'trim'
3. Funky house
4. Paralegal
5. The Grammys
6. Edo
7. Whoopi Goldberg
8. Eastpak
9. Yellow
10. Nikah
11. Tapas
12. Atomic
13. Amsterdam
14. *Becoming*
15. Shito

NOT-SO-GENERAL KNOWLEDGE

ROUND 30

1. Black theatre
2. Martin Luther King Jr Day
3. Octavia E. Butler
4. On a bottle of sun cream
5. Twice
6. Google
7. Moira
8. Egypt
9. Cleo Sol/*Mother*
10. Red
11. Koeksister
12. 99
13. 'You Either Love It or Hate It'
14. Alesha Dixon, Su-Elise Nash and Sabrina Washington
15. As Seen on Screen

NOT-SO-GENERAL KNOWLEDGE

ROUND 31

1. *Ctrl*
2. Roasts
3. The Torah
4. *Sounds of My World*
5. Penguin Random House
6. Fortune 500
7. Françoise Bettencourt Meyers
8. Matthew
9. 'Soft life'
10. Kendrick Lamar
11. *Love in Colour*
12. Pan-African
13. Tottenham Hotspur Stadium
14. Mint leaves
15. Zinoleesky/'Kilofeshe'

NOT-SO-GENERAL KNOWLEDGE

ROUND 32

1. B613
2. Plantain
3. *Say Your Mind*
4. Rum
5. *Dele Weds Destiny*
6. Stomach
7. Perfume
8. Virgil Abloh
9. Mali
10. 'Lift Every Voice and Sing'
11. Holi
12. Bouff Daddy
13. Coco Sarel
14. Porsha Williams
15. 2022

NOT-SO-GENERAL KNOWLEDGE

ROUND 33

1. Tate Modern
2. Roti
3. Morgan Freeman
4. Naming ceremony
5. Five
6. O levels
7. Gospel
8. Bravo
9. Figs
10. Ms Banks
11. House of CB
12. Zucchini
13. *25*
14. Nose
15. Jo Malone

NOT-SO-GENERAL KNOWLEDGE

ROUND 34

1. Oceania
2. JLS
3. Daniel
4. *It Was Good Until It Wasn't*/Kehlani
5. Corporate social responsibility
6. Soup
7. Love of My Life
8. Ms. Dynamite
9. Five
10. Camille Parks
11. Namibia
12. Jade LB
13. Bambi
14. Benefit Cosmetics
15. *You People*

NOT-SO-GENERAL KNOWLEDGE

ROUND 35

1. Psalms
2. 32
3. 66,000 miles
4. Cobbler
5. Oyinkan Braithwaite
6. Sierra Leone
7. 2005
8. Boeing
9. 2007
10. Wind speed and wind pressure
11. *Paid in Full*
12. 12
13. Labrinth
14. Northern Line
15. Wii Sports

NOT-SO-GENERAL KNOWLEDGE

ROUND 36

1. 2023
2. King Solomon
3. BZD
4. Universal Media Disc
5. Glaciologist
6. Tems
7. Red
8. 36
9. True
10. Carolina Reaper
11. Shake/shaking my head
12. Muslims
13. Dishoom
14. Comedy
15. Atheist

NOT-SO-GENERAL KNOWLEDGE

ROUND 37

1. Fourth
2. *Let It Shine*
3. Bollywood
4. Two
5. Surah
6. Farai London
7. DJ Maphorisa and Kabza de Small
8. Negroni
9. *An American Marriage*
10. Drum and bass
11. H&M group
12. French
13. Kwame and Terry
14. Unknown T
15. Omo Baba Olowo

NOT-SO-GENERAL KNOWLEDGE

ROUND 38

1. Plantain
2. Beyoncé, Britney Spears, P!nk and Enrique Iglesias
3. Democratic Republic of the Congo and Republic of Congo
4. Psalms
5. Prime Meridian
6. The dawa cocktail
7. OFSTED
8. Kissing
9. Lizzo
10. 'I don't want to eat poison'
11. Simbi (or Simbiatu)
12. Friday 13th
13. Mandasi
14. Two
15. 'Teach Me'

NOT-SO-GENERAL KNOWLEDGE

ROUND 39

1. Abstinence from alcohol
2. Black Sherif
3. 1996
4. Not safe for work
5. Lays
6. Gentrification
7. Fried yam and plantain
8. Bree Runway
9. Mediums
10. Boubou
11. The Ten Commandments
12. Jazmine Sullivan/*Heaux Tales*
13. Milk
14. 'If you know, you know'
15. Camille Grammer

NOT-SO-GENERAL KNOWLEDGE

ROUND 40

1. Pasodoble
2. December
3. Chidera Eggerue
4. 38
5. Asexual
6. A wedding
7. Insanity workout
8. South Africa
9. Make-up brands
10. 2006
11. North
12. 'Close to You'
13. British
14. Ethiopia
15. Attorneys

NOT-SO-GENERAL KNOWLEDGE

ROUND 41

1. Featured in the TV series *Insecure*
2. Sadza
3. Arinzé Kene
4. Doula
5. 28
6. South Africa
7. Nothing
8. Loubrand Studios
9. Casa Amor
10. Lauryn Hill
11. Gin
12. Zora Neale Hurston
13. Ctrl + 9
14. Sanskrit
15. Upcycling

NOT-SO-GENERAL KNOWLEDGE

ROUND 42

1. Red Ring of Death
2. Three
3. Asamoah Gyan
4. Baobab
5. Epistle to Philemon
6. New York
7. Aston Martin DB9 Volante
8. Pip
9. A magnetic compass
10. *A Visible Man*
11. Mai tai
12. £200
13. AFCON/African Cup Of Nations
14. Dreams
15. Monaco

NOT-SO-GENERAL KNOWLEDGE

ROUND 43

1. Richard Blackwood
2. Electronic Entertainment Expo
3. 2012
4. Fanta
5. Magazines
6. Dating
7. David Beckham
8. Bamako
9. Teaching
10. Dave/*Psychodrama*
11. Jerusalem
12. *Everything Is Love*
13. 1982
14. Pharrell Williams
15. Black Gals Livin'

NOT-SO-GENERAL KNOWLEDGE

ROUND 44

1. Ag
2. Make the sun, moon and stars
3. Shooting incident
4. Google, Netflix, Amazon
5. Speaking Parseltongue
6. John McCain
7. Jouvert
8. The Knowledge
9. Banana
10. Flock together
11. Yahoo Boy No Laptop
12. Global majority
13. Guadeloupe, Martinique, St Barts and St Martin
14. Carol
15. Nine

NOT-SO-GENERAL KNOWLEDGE

ROUND 45

1. Joe
2. Cupid
3. Stomach
4. Dark 'n' stormy
5. House plant
6. Soca
7. Three points
8. Fisayo
9. Xenophobia
10. Couscous
11. Taurus
12. BBC Four and CBBC
13. Aloe vera
14. Bravo
15. Fulani

NOT-SO-GENERAL KNOWLEDGE

ROUND 46

1. The electric slide
2. Shot of tequila followed by a shot of pineapple juice
3. Cancer
4. 'Warm'/K-Trap
5. African American Vernacular English
6. Ellie Goulding
7. Venus
8. Dream Weekend
9. Mustard
10. Ground roasted peanuts
11. Nappy Boy Radio
12. Milk
13. Keke Palmer
14. US
15. Wretch 32

NOT-SO-GENERAL KNOWLEDGE

ROUND 47

1. Coriander
2. Candice Brathwaite
3. Patagonia
4. Corlys Velaryon
5. Brampton Manor
6. *Send Them to Coventry*/ Pa Salieu
7. Pro Evolution Soccer
8. Maya Angelou
9. Liberia or Ethiopia
10. Channel U
11. Pineapple
12. Malcolm X
13. Brixton Splash
14. Rihanna
15. February

NOT-SO-GENERAL KNOWLEDGE

ROUND 48

1. Emmy, Grammy, Oscar and Tony Awards
2. Getting engaged
3. $10,000
4. Historically Black colleges and universities
5. Nine Ladies Dancing
6. Beans/black-eyed peas
7. Mile High Club
8. Arcangelo
9. A pickle
10. Mecca
11. Sugar/sugar cane
12. Paris
13. Bar mitzvah
14. Toni, Maya, Lynn and Joan
15. Donald Glover

NOT-SO-GENERAL KNOWLEDGE

ROUND 49

1. George W. Bush
2. *Don't Be a Menace to South Central While Drinking Your Juice in the Hood*
3. In the beginning
4. Sex on the beach
5. PK Humble
6. Pasta
7. Bishop
8. Skrapz and Nines
9. Whisky
10. Gina Coladangelo
11. Jumu'ah
12. Jackie Aina
13. Contraceptive pill
14. Yvonne Orji
15. Leather

NOT-SO-GENERAL KNOWLEDGE

ROUND 50

1. Brent
2. Michael, Gabriel, Apollyon/Abaddon
3. Wordle
4. Uganda
5. Super Bowl Sunday
6. Fritz
7. Southern Africa
8. Helmet
9. Proverb
10. Damilare Kuku
11. Tears of Caesar
12. Ama
13. Rice
14. Pink
15. Europe, Middle East, Africa

NOT-SO-GENERAL KNOWLEDGE

ROUND 51

1. The Adenugas
2. Royal flush
3. Lot's wife
4. *No Behaviour Podcast*
5. Richard Mofe-Damijo
6. Nitrous oxide (N_2O)
7. 31
8. 5-day pass
9. Wudu
10. Lyanna Mormont
11. Kansas or Kentucky
12. Air
13. 13
14. *Chasing Summer*/SiR
15. Gem

NOT-SO-GENERAL KNOWLEDGE

ROUND 52

1. P Diddy
2. Paparazzi
3. Pat McGrath
4. Barty Crease
5. Laureate
6. Duppy
7. Tequila
8. Goat
9. Salmon
10. Jungle skank
11. 'Monster'
12. The 50 US states
13. 'Hello'
14. June
15. M&S Mojito

NOT-SO-GENERAL KNOWLEDGE

ROUND 53

1. Aston Martin
2. Olusegun Obasanjo
3. Ivy League
4. Romans
5. Octagonal
6. Panama Papers
7. Skinny/Slim
8. Dusty Depot
9. Democratic Republic of Congo and Republic of Congo
10. Mango
11. Ganesha/Ganapati
12. Nike
13. Baby mother
14. Three months
15. Chip

NOT-SO-GENERAL KNOWLEDGE

ROUND 54

1. *Roots*/NSG
2. Marriage, women and family
3. Usain Bolt, Stormzy, Yaya Touré
4. 16
5. Shabbat/Sabbath/Shabbos
6. Uganda
7. Eight-Tails, Gyūki
8. Fenchurch Street, Liverpool Street, Marylebone and King's Cross
9. Gumbo
10. Hermes
11. Married
12. Chapman
13. Scorpio, Pisces and Cancer
14. A species of frog
15. 'One Dance'

NOT-SO-GENERAL KNOWLEDGE

ROUND 55

1. Islington
2. Vanilla Ice
3. Brain
4. Moscow mule
5. Big Brovaz
6. Peckham
7. Morehouse College
8. 'Charmaine'
9. Lil Wayne, Gudda Gudda, Nicki Minaj, Drake, Tyga, Jae Millz, Lloyd
10. King's Cross
11. *Making the Band*
12. *Now That's What I Call Music*
13. Zadie Smith
14. Central Cee
15. Misha B

NOT-SO-GENERAL KNOWLEDGE

ROUND 56

1. Odun
2. Pilates
3. Storm Eunice
4. Six
5. 96 years old
6. Six
7. Cost of living crisis
8. Low vibrational
9. Album of the Year
10. Pussy and mimosas
11. Tiffany & Co.
12. Burna Boy
13. bell hooks
14. Severus Snape
15. Kurt Geiger

ARE YOU SMARTER THAN A 10-YEAR-OLD?

ROUND 1

1. Chlorophyll
2. Amphibians
3. Elmer
4. Manifesto
5. I love you
6. 32 teeth
7. Warthog
8. Examination boards
9. 41 years ago. $3(54 - x) = 80 - x$, $162 - 3x = 80 - x$, $162 - 80 = 3x - x$, $82 = 2x$, $x = 41$
10. False
11. Compass
12. Amarillo
13. XXII
14. The cabinet
15. 2 hours 24 minutes

ARE YOU SMARTER THAN A 10-YEAR-OLD?

ROUND 2

1. Danish, Maltese, Somali
2. 1 January 1901
3. Invertebrate
4. Roald Dahl
5. Insulators
6. England, Scotland, Wales and Northern Ireland
7. Fe
8. Ctrl + K
9. 44
10. Homophones
11. Ancient life forms
12. 'What's your name?'
13. Kneecap
14. 24
15. Omnivore

ARE YOU SMARTER THAN A 10-YEAR-OLD?

ROUND 3

1. 12
2. Vixen
3. £12,000
4. 118
5. Creed, colour, name
6. 350
7. Earth
8. Oxen
9. 14
10. Beats per minute (BPM)
11. 720
12. 1,000
13. East
14. 20
15. 7

ARE YOU SMARTER THAN A 10-YEAR-OLD?

ROUND 4

1. Rhythm and blues
2. Hemispheres
3. Gaggle
4. 1,600
5. Quebec
6. CCXIV
7. 585
8. Ibuprofen
9. 0
10. Solid, liquid and gas
11. Stanley Yelnats
12. 1,800
13. Charles Dickens
14. Digestive and circulatory systems
15. 24

ARE YOU SMARTER THAN A 10-YEAR-OLD?

ROUND 5

1. John Agard
2. 65
3. Blue whale
4. Every five years
5. 2, 3, 5, 7, 11
6. Point, evidence, explain
7. *'J'habite à Londres'*
8. 201
9. 7
10. The break of day
11. Mannequin
12. Scalene and equilateral
13. Antarctica
14. 141
15. Square root

ARE YOU SMARTER THAN A 10-YEAR-OLD?

ROUND 6

1. Nauseous
2. Soluble
3. Horse
4. ¼
5. Councils
6. Decibels
7. Aslan
8. 5p
9. Brain
10. 11
11. James and Lily Potter
12. Albuquerque
13. Nine
14. Mitosis
15. Renaissance

ARE YOU SMARTER THAN A 10-YEAR-OLD?

ROUND 7

1. 60
2. Condensation
3. 35 per cent
4. Curley's wife
5. Vote in a general election.
6. DR Congo
7. 30
8. Numerator
9. Moose
10. 15
11. Twelve
12. Conscientious
13. Two
14. Bigger and biggest
15. 20 minutes

ARE YOU SMARTER THAN A 10-YEAR-OLD?

ROUND 8

1. *Knife Edge*
2. Great Lakes
3. Harper Lee
4. 4.17pm
5. Blood
6. South-west
7. Thursday
8. Personal, social, health and economic
9. 10,101
10. Furniture
11. Trapezium
12. Most
13. Woodwind
14. 10 stone
15. Photosynthesis

ARE YOU SMARTER THAN A 10-YEAR-OLD?

ROUND 9

1. Four years
2. Herbivore
3. *Harry Potter and the Deathly Hallows*
4. Eight
5. Blue, yellow and red
6. Cock/rooster
7. Nine
8. 2 and 11
9. Pb
10. Broadsheet
11. Agnostic
12. True
13. House of Commons and House of Lords
14. 8 March
15. Union Jack/Union Flag

ARE YOU SMARTER THAN A 10-YEAR-OLD?

ROUND 10

1. Fuchsia
2. 1614
3. Poetry
4. Four (121 , 144, 169, 196)
5. Purple
6. Ne
7. 480
8. Mare
9. Labour Party
10. Mercury
11. 12
12. Member of Parliament
13. Canine
14. Reptile
15. Dipsy

A QUESTION OF SPORT

ROUND 1

1. Burnley
2. Naomi Osaka
3. Wrestling
4. Twice
5. Christian Coleman and Justin Gatlin
6. Lionel Messi
7. Ada Hegerberg
8. Los Angeles Lakers
9. Netball
10. Neymar
11. Sue Barker
12. Linford Christie
13. EFL League One
14. Jude Bellingham, Bukayo Saka, Raheem Sterling, Marcus Rashford
15. Paris

A QUESTION OF SPORT

ROUND 2

1. Rugby union
2. 2002
3. Rio Ferdinand
4. Madison Square Garden, New York City
5. Pelé
6. Cue
7. UK
8. Boxing
9. South Africa
10. Russell Westbrook
11. 2010
12. Cricket
13. *Slay in Your Lane*, the title of her co-written book
14. José Mourinho
15. Bobsleigh

A QUESTION OF SPORT

ROUND 3

1. Cori 'Coco' Gauff
2. England
3. France
4. Video assistant referee
5. The Walls of Jericho
6. Riyad Mahrez
7. Martial art
8. 200 metres
9. Robin van Persie
10. Dikembe Mutombo
11. Kelly Cates
12. Southend United
13. Candace Parker
14. Trampolining
15. Sporting Lisbon

A QUESTION OF SPORT

ROUND 4

1. Thrilla in Manilla
2. Japan
3. Golf
4. 1986
5. Stephen A. Smith
6. Six
7. Eni Aluko
8. Triple H
9. Strawberries and cream
10. Shelly-Ann Fraser-Pryce
11. Woolwich
12. Romelu Lukaku
13. Simone Biles
14. Scoring one goal with the left foot, one with the right and one with a header
15. Kelly Holmes

A QUESTION OF SPORT

ROUND 5

1. Israel Adesanya
2. Two players: goal attack (GA) and goal shooter (GS)
3. John Mosley
4. Windrush Day
5. Kofi Kingston
6. 'Stone Cold' Steve Austin
7. 11
8. Mesut Özil
9. Barbra Banda
10. Cricket
11. Dirk Nowitzki/Germany
12. Uruguay
13. 100 metres butterfly
14. Darts
15. Thierry Henry

A QUESTION OF SPORT

ROUND 6

1. Sheffield
2. 'Bring the cup back home'
3. Didier Drogba
4. Abedi Pele
5. Brazil
6. Chris Eubanks and Nigel Benn
7. Scoring 'zero'
8. UFC welterweight title
9. 15
10. Ronaldinho's crossbar challenge
11. 2016
12. Jordan Poole
13. Pastor
14. White Hart Lane
15. Serve

A QUESTION OF SPORT

ROUND 7

1. Ligue 1
2. Football
3. Los Angeles Lakers
4. Germany
5. Carmelita Jeter
6. Aberdeen
7. Liverpool and Everton
8. Long jump, heptathlon, 10,000 metres
9. Philadelphia Eagles and Kansas City Chiefs
10. Clay
11. Kylian Mbappé
12. Tennis
13. Wimbledon
14. 97
15. Argentina

A QUESTION OF SPORT

ROUND 8

1. 1992
2. UConn
3. National Football League
4. The All Blacks
5. New York Liberty
6. Tea-drinking action
7. Germany
8. Derby County
9. 11
10. Four
11. Alex Iwobi
12. Brazil
13. Derek Redmond
14. Most valuable player
15. Ellen White

A QUESTION OF SPORT

ROUND 9

1. Usain Bolt, Yohan Blake, Michael Frater, Nesta Carter
2. 2012
3. Fenerbahçe
4. Germany
5. Andy Murray
6. Seven
7. Tennis
8. Buster Douglas
9. QPR
10. Canadian
11. Kylian Mbappé
12. Monaco
13. Inter Miami
14. Women's Super League
15. Barcelona

A QUESTION OF SPORT

ROUND 10

1. Colorado
2. Portland Thorns
3. Belgian
4. Manchester City
5. Steve Kerr
6. Two
7. Shelly-Ann Fraser-Price
8. Glasgow Rangers
9. 48 minutes
10. 32
11. New York
12. Germany
13. 12 players
14. Charlton Athletic
15. Rafael Nadal

A QUESTION OF SPORT

ROUND 11

1. Portsmouth
2. Jamaica
3. Philadelphia 76ers
4. Eastern and Western
5. Five
6. 100 metres and 200 metres
7. A turkey
8. Rihanna
9. Deuce
10. Seven
11. Liverpool
12. Novak Djokovic
13. Charlotte Hornets
14. Sachin Tendulkar
15. Long jump

A QUESTION OF SPORT

ROUND 12

1. George Foreman and Muhammad Ali
2. 2004
3. Australian Open
4. Patrick Vieira
5. Lionel Messi
6. Triathlon
7. Sunderland
8. Bayern Munich and Borussia Dortmund
9. Alexis Putellas
10. Venus Williams
11. Michael Jackson
12. An Olympic gold medal in singles tennis
13. Unai Emery
14. Nico Rosberg
15. 20

A QUESTION OF SPORT

ROUND 13

1. Florence Griffith Joyner
2. Arsenal
3. Kylian Mbappé
4. Serena Williams
5. Nigeria
6. Sunderland
7. Geno Auriemma
8. Sue Barker
9. Real Madrid
10. 23
11. Tennis
12. The Detroit Pistons
13. Ryan Giggs
14. Sylvia Fowles
15. The Super Bowl

A QUESTION OF SPORT

ROUND 14

1. 2015/16
2. Taekwondo
3. 5 + 24 = 29
4. Elland Road
5. Nigeria and Ghana
6. Boston Celtics
7. US
8. Four. (Everton (twice), Manchester United, Derby County and D.C. United)
9. Baseball (MLB)
10. Dressage (equestrian)
11. 2–1
12. Bobby Charlton
13. Crystal Palace and Brighton Hove Albion
14. Porto and Inter Milan
15. Australian Open

A QUESTION OF SPORT

ROUND 15

1. 30
2. Portugal
3. Tim Cahill
4. Philadelphia 76ers
5. Pierre-Emerick Aubameyang, Mo Salah and Sadio Mane
6. PSG
7. Leah Williamson
8. Football
9. Bayern Munich
10. Zlatan Ibrahimović
11. 25
12. 2003
13. Cristiano Ronaldo
14. Bahamas
15. Blake Griffin

A QUESTION OF SPORT

ROUND 16

1. Aston Villa
2. 82
3. 9–0
4. Steffi Graf
5. Glasgow Rangers and Celtic
6. World Wrestling Entertainment
7. Two
8. Heptathlon
9. Vivianne Miedema
10. Emiliano Martinez
11. Senegal
12. Twice
13. Real Madrid and Inter Milan
14. American
15. Arsène Wenger

A QUESTION OF SPORT

ROUND 17

1. Enzo Fernández
2. Sarina Wiegman
3. Crystal Palace
4. Manchester United
5. Fleetwood Town
6. Cardiff City and Swansea City
7. Andre Agassi
8. Miroslav Klose
9. Women's National Basketball Association
10. 400 metres
11. Miami Heat and Orlando Magic
12. Manchester United
13. Iceland
14. Juan Martín del Potro
15. Wimbledon

A QUESTION OF SPORT

ROUND 18

1. Liverpool
2. Paris
3. Fulham
4. Celtic
5. Three
6. Football
7. Small forward and shooting guard
8. Alan Shearer, Harry Kane and Wayne Rooney
9. Margaret Court
10. Ice hockey
11. Andre Agassi
12. Red Bull
13. Barcelona 3–1 Manchester United
14. Real Madrid and Barcelona
15. California

A QUESTION OF SPORT

ROUND 19

1. Jamie Vardy
2. Carlo Ancelotti
3. Egypt
4. Slovenia
5. Golden State Warriors
6. BMX Supercross
7. Pommel horse
8. South Africa
9. South Africa
10. Dina Asher-Smith
11. Serbia
12. National Football League
13. Beth Tweddle
14. Crystal Palace
15. January

A QUESTION OF SPORT

ROUND 20

1. Beth Mead
2. Sadio Mané
3. Fred Perry
4. 12
5. Angel City
6. Vivianne Miedema
7. February
8. Bill Russell
9. 7
10. 9.69 seconds
11. Ian Rush
12. Australia
13. Wrexham
14. Teddy Sheringham
15. Boxing

A QUESTION OF SPORT

ROUND 21

1. Kobe Bryant
2. Mainz and Borussia Dortmund
3. Evander Holyfield
4. Darts
5. Chicago Bulls
6. Petr Čech
7. Pittsburgh Steelers
8. Chelsea
9. Nottingham Forest
10. Three (Miami Heat, Cleveland Cavaliers, Los Angeles Lakers)
11. Five
12. Middlesbrough
13. Phil Taylor
14. Southampton
15. *High School Musical*

UK GARAGE ROUND

1. Artful Dodger
2. Master of ceremonies
3. Preditah
4. Coronet Theatre
5. DJ Luck and MC Neat
6. 2001
7. Twice as Nice
8. 'Lights On'
9. Pay As U Go Cartel
10. 'Sweet Like Chocolate'/ Shanks & Bigfoot
11. Three
12. Garage house
13. 'Crazy Love'/MJ Cole
14. Funky house and dubstep
15. 'Baby Cakes'

GRIME ROUND

1. *Treddin' on Thin Ice*
2. Nines
3. Lord of the Mics
4. Roll Deep
5. Mercury Prize
6. 140
7. £80
8. 'Pied Piper'
9. Carlos
10. DJ Target
11. Mist
12. Shaybo
13. Petrol station
14. Devilman
15. Big Narstie

POP CULTURE ROUND

1. Dr. Rainbow Johnson
2. *Love and Compromise/*
   Mahalia
3. Cristiano Ronaldo
4. 'The Boy Is Mine'
5. Clothing brand
6. 15
7. Penelope, Mason and
   Reign
8. Gnarls Barkley
9. Manchester
10. *Good Morning America*
11. *The Weakest Link*
12. Snoop Dogg
13. Nike
14. D Double E
15. N-Dubz

FILM AND TV

ROUND 1

1. Steven Avery
2. *Sex Education*
3. To marry a divorced
   woman
4. The Full Counter
5. Miss Danbury
6. Netflix
7. *This Is Us*
8. Jellyfish
9. Spain
10. Tracey
11. Mona the Vampire
12. *We Got Y'all*
13. Thandiwe Newton
14. The Sunken Place
15. *Joseline's Cabaret*

FILM AND TV

ROUND 2

1. *Moonlight*
2. *Modern Family*
3. 2023
4. Darius Lovehall and Nina Mosley
5. Lady Leshurr
6. Ghana
7. Aml Ameen
8. Nakia
9. *Are You the One?*
10. California
11. ITV2
12. *EastEnders*
13. *The Only Way Is Essex*
14. 1998
15. Jamie Foxx

FILM AND TV

ROUND 3

1. 3 Mills Studios
2. John Singleton
3. Ashley Walters
4. Missandei
5. *The Matrix*
6. British Academy of Film and Television Arts
7. *Waiting to Exhale*
8. Peckham and Brixton
9. Chiwetel Ejiofor
10. BBC One
11. Robert 'Granddad' Freeman
12. Netflix and Amazon Prime Video
13. *Get Out*
14. 14
15. *Casualty*

ANIME ROUND

1. Jet, which gives him immense speed
2. Ego
3. Nezu
4. Team Z
5. 300
6. 6 November 2022
7. Tokyo City Esperion FC
8. Permetation, which enables him to become intangible, letting him pass through any tangible matter (phasing through walls, etc.)
9. Senzu beans
10. One day
11. Katsuki Bakugo
12. Cart Titan
13. Body Improvement Club
14. Spy Wars
15. Jormungand

MARVEL ROUND

1. An undisclosed illness
2. MIT
3. Six
4. *Iron Man 2*
5. Nebula and Gamora
6. Bucky
7. Mysterio
8. Left
9. Trevor Noah
10. Exposure to gamma radiation
11. Hela
12. Michael B. Jordan
13. Iron Man
14. Vibranium, steel alloy and Proto-Adamantium
15. Thor

FASHION ROUND

1. Kai Collective
2. Telfar Clemens
3. Moschino
4. Crocs
5. Air Max 95s
6. Damon Dash and Jay-Z
7. StockX
8. Ralph Lauren
9. Lollipop
10. Adidas
11. Paris, New York, London and Milan
12. £50
13. 'Bust down'
14. Italy
15. Billionaire Boys Club

WHO AM I?

ROUND 1

1. Wretch 32
2. Hope Powell
3. Fekky
4. Patricia Bright
5. Chunkz
6. Olaudah Equiano
7. Paul Stephenson
8. Trevor McDonald
9. Julie Adenuga
10. Denise Lewis
11. Ashley Walters
12. Louis Theroux
13. Sophie Okonedo
14. Charlie Williams
15. Dreya Mac

WHO AM I?

ROUND 2

1. Ghetts
2. D Double E
3. Sade
4. Jamal Edwards
5. Akala
6. Marcus Rashford
7. Kanya King
8. David Lammy
9. Linford Christie
10. Micah Richards
11. Alison Hammond
12. Zadie Smith
13. Zeze Millz
14. Tinchy Stryder
15. Yasmin Evans

TWITTER AND TIKTOK ROUND

1. Zola
2. Sunday
3. 'Ladies, shall we have some fun?'
4. Cat Burns
5. 21 December
6. Musical.ly
7. Oui Oui Twitter
8. Non-player character
9. Twitter Circle
10. Dating and relationships
11. Marriage
12. Rihanna and Teyana Taylor
13. #talkswithash
14. Food reviews
15. Ginger/auburn

MY WIFE AND KIDS ROUND

1. Five
2. Jay is pregnant
3. 16
4. Meagan Good
5. Tony
6. Trucking company
7. Pie
8. Aretha
9. Marie
10. The Hoos
11. The Bye Bye Birdie
12. Aloysius
13. *Romeo and Juliet*
14. Dr. Bouche
15. 'Wisdom'

BLACK HISTORY

ROUND 1

1. 1963
2. Martin Luther King Jr
3. Charlene White
4. Black Curriculum
5. Attend Oxford University
6. UK Black Pride
7. Ghana
8. Sandra Bland
9. Tilbury Docks
10. Millions
11. Newcastle
12. Olaudah Equiano
13. Black Panther Party
14. St James' Church
15. Jasmine Thompson

BLACK HISTORY

ROUND 2

1. Jack Leslie
2. 'Do You Mind' by Crazy Cousinz
3. Reni Eddo-Lodge
4. Banksy
5. 1960
6. Castleford Tigers
7. Malorie Blackman
8. *Chewing Gum*
9. 2003
10. Paul Stephenson
11. Rochdale
12. Bow, east London
13. Chinua Achebe
14. 2019
15. 1957

BLACK HISTORY

ROUND 3

1. Arthur Wharton
2. Ryan Calais Cameron
3. Desmond's
4. 2011
5. Mary Seacole
6. Daniel Kaluuya
7. 2008
8. Jammer's
9. Gil Scott-Heron
10. 2011
11. Linford Christie
12. Fela Kuti
13. 1984
14. Chimamanda Ngozi Adichie
15. Dina Asher-Smith

BLACK HISTORY

ROUND 4

1. Katarina Johnson-Thompson
2. Queen Charlotte
3. Boxing
4. Barbara Blake Hannah
5. ITV
6. 2006
7. 2008
8. Rapman
9. Jamaica
10. 1962
11. 4.2
12. Barbados
13. 2017
14. Clint
15. Hope Powell

BLACK HISTORY

ROUND 5

1. Pat McGrath
2. Robert Nesta Marley
3. Swimming
4. Belgium
5. 1990
6. Tobi Oredein
7. Ainsley Harriott
8. 1906
9. Wiley
10. Patricia Bright
11. Vybz Kartel
12. 1962
13. 1990
14. Steve McQueen
15. 1976

BLACK HISTORY

ROUND 6

1. Patrice Lumumba
2. 1967
3. 'One Dance'
4. *Babylon*
5. Frankie Knuckles
6. Menelik Shabazz
7. Mo Farah
8. Athens 2004
9. Jme and Skepta
10. Edward Enninful
11. 2003
12. 1966
13. Neil Kenlock
14. David and Jojo Sonubi
15. Kwame Nkrumah

BLACK HISTORY

ROUND 7

1. Idris Elba
2. Charlotte Mensah
3. 2016
4. Trouble
5. 2001
6. Kenya Hunt
7. Craig David
8. 2018
9. Kanya King
10. 1834
11. Mansa Musa
12. 1991
13. Lagos
14. Madam C. J. Walker
15. Beyoncé

BLACK HISTORY

ROUND 8

1. 30 June
2. Matt 'Sketchy' Thorne, Pierre Godson-Amamoo, Koby 'Posty' Hagan
3. Hattie McDaniel
4. Sidney Poitier
5. James Baldwin
6. Dahomey tribe
7. DJ Abrantee
8. The death of Mark Duggan
9. 20,000
10. Freetown and Libreville
11. Lagos
12. 2013
13. *Home Sweet Home*
14. Naomi Campbell
15. Levi Roots

BLACK HISTORY

ROUND 9

1. Lauryn Hill
2. 2019
3. Tim Campbell
4. James Brown, Little Richard, Sam Cooke, Chuck Berry, Fats Domino, Ray Charles
5. Fela Kuti
6. Zimbabwe in 1980
7. Trinidad and Tobago
8. Lewis Hamilton
9. Walter Tull
10. Dame Kelly Holmes
11. Heptathlon
12. 2016
13. Khadijah Mellah
14. Jourdan Dunn
15. Sheila Johnson

BLACK HISTORY

ROUND 10

1. Berry Gordy
2. 1993
3. 'I Will Always Love'/ Whitney Houston
4. *Awkward Black Girl*
5. Halle Berry
6. Tina Turner
7. Steve McQueen
8. 2013
9. Usain Bolt
10. Princess Tiana
11. Jim Crow Laws
12. 22 April
13. Lauryn Hill
14. 2009
15. Harry Edward

BLACK HISTORY

ROUND 11

1. Tiger Woods
2. Tinie Tempah/Dumi Oburota
3. Sheryl Lee Ralph
4. Jay-Z
5. Solange and Beyoncé
6. Quincy Jones
7. 1980
8. William Arthur Lewis
9. *Atlanta*
10. 1954
11. Huey P. Newton and Bobby Seale
12. Muhammad Ali
13. Jan Matzeliger
14. Guion Bluford
15. Rhythm and poetry

BLACK HISTORY

ROUND 12

1. New York
2. Porn star martini
3. Kiss 100
4. 1993
5. Mali
6. Thomas Sankara
7. Aretha Franklin
8. Sister Rosetta Tharpe
9. 2006
10. 1791
11. France
12. King Leopold II
13. Kunta Kinte
14. *12 Years a Slave*
15. *Small Axe*

BLACK HISTORY

ROUND 13

1. Tupac Shakur
2. 1985
3. *Moonlight*
4. Tarana Burke
5. Spike Lee
6. Steve Harvey
7. Kamala Harris
8. Virgil Abloh
9. Dame Elizabeth Anionwu
10. Tendai Moyo and Ugo Agbai
11. Shakaila Forbes-Bell
12. Nella Rose
13. 1935
14. Wallace Fard Muhammad
15. *The Receipts*

BLACK HISTORY

ROUND 14

1. Zimbabwe
2. Muhammad Ali
3. Ghana
4. Jerry Rawlings
5. EndSARS
6. 1968
7. 1958
8. Audre Lorde
9. Contributing essential mathematics to the first American space flight and the Apollo 11 mission
10. Marcus Garvey
11. Harold Moody
12. Paul Stephenson
13. Doreen Lawrence
14. Baroness Scotland
15. 6 March

BLACK HISTORY

ROUND 15

1. 2020
2. Maggie Aderin-Pocock
3. Mangrove Nine
4. Princess Adenrele Ademola or Omo-Oba Adenrele
5. Angela Davis
6. Kimberlé Williams Crenshaw
7. Margaret Busby
8. 1980
9. 1970
10. Sons
11. Montgomery, Alabama
12. Three days
13. Black People's Day of Action march of 1981
14. Val McCalla
15. Claudia Jones

BLACK HISTORY

ROUND 16

1. 1998
2. Mary Seacole
3. Walter Tull
4. Nelson Mandela
5. Toni Morrison
6. Bernie Grant Arts Centre
7. 1961
8. Frantz Fanon
9. Rodney King
10. 'Strange Fruit' by Billie Holiday
11. Mau Mau Uprising
12. The Supremes
13. 1993
14. Maya Angelou
15. Bob Marley

1980S ROUND

1. *Coming 2 America*
2. 1981
3. 'Saving All My Love for You'
4. Daley Thompson
5. Conservative Party
6. The Whispers
7. Michael Jackson
8. Incitement to Racial Hatred Act
9. The wedding of Prince Charles and Lady Diana Spencer
10. South Africa
11. Ian Beale
12. Bernie Grant
13. Soul II Soul
14. Uganda
15. *Can't Slow Down*

1990S

ROUND 1

1. 3 Lil Women
2. Because you never know what you're gonna get
3. Will Smith/*Men in Black* and *Independence Day*
4. *Rush Hour*
5. Stu and Didi Pickles
6. Mike Tyson bit Evander Holyfield's ear
7. The jungle gym
8. Refugees
9. *Hey Arnold!*
10. Greg Wuliger
11. Mr Blobby
12. Opal Fruits
13. *Scooby-Doo*
14. En Vogue
15. *Blind Date*

1990S

ROUND 2

1. Washington, DC
2. Panda Pops
3. Chris Ofili
4. 'Trial of the Century'
5. Atlanta
6. Cleopatra
7. The Good Friday Agreement
8. Seal
9. 'I Will Always Love You'
10. Slinky
11. London, England and Napa, California
12. For Us, By Us
13. Des'ree
14. Iraq
15. A Bug A Boo

2000S

ROUND 1

1. A watch
2. *Smile*
3. Basil Brush
4. Y2K
5. BlackBerry phone
6. *Corneil & Bernie*
7. Rimmel
8. Fat Joe, Remy Ma and Terror Squad
9. 2000
10. Smokey Bars TV
11. Five
12. Britney Spears
13. CBBC
14. 'Smelly cat, smelly cat'
15. Sean John

2000S

ROUND 2

1. American Music Awards
2. *That's So Raven*
3. Nickelodeon
4. *Mean Girls*
5. Bebo
6. Frankee
7. Channel 4
8. Channel AKA and Starz TV
9. Facebook
10. *The Office*
11. Hand
12. *8 Mile*
13. *Iron Man*
14. 50
15. *The Da Vinci Code*

2000S

ROUND 3

1. *College Dropout*
2. Missy Elliott
3. Chick and duck
4. Friday
5. Funky Dee
6. *The Simple Life*
7. SimNation
8. LaTavia Roberson and LeToya Luckett
9. 1998
10. Zoe Slater
11. Fundamental 03
12. P Diddy
13. Gordon Brown
14. SmarterChild
15. Lehman Brothers

2010S ROUND

1. 2014
2. Capital Xtra
3. Stooshe
4. 2013 and 2014
5. Third
6. ALS
7. Gordon Brown
8. Rizzle Kicks
9. iPad
10. 21 December 2012
11. Black and blue/white and gold
12. Change their skin colour
13. *Common Sense*
14. Arab Spring
15. Six seconds

GEOGRAPHY

ROUND 1

1. London and Leeds
2. New Cross Gate overground station
3. Accra
4. Jamaica
5. Dalston Lane
6. Out of town
7. Liberia
8. Japan and Jordan
9. *Grand Theft Auto*
10. Antigua
11. Three
12. Saint Lucia
13. Uganda
14. Newcastle
15. Leicester

GEOGRAPHY

ROUND 2

1. Madagascar
2. Algeria
3. Tanzania
4. Antigua and Barbuda
5. Birmingham
6. Nassau
7. Malawi
8. Trinidad and Tobago
9. Lesotho
10. Curaçao
11. Ghana
12. Albania and United Kingdom
13. Togo
14. Thailand
15. Manchester

GEOGRAPHY

ROUND 3

1. Newham
2. 76
3. 2011
4. Cuba
5. Maasai
6. Chad
7. Grafton Street
8. Cyprus
9. Compton
10. Mindless Behaviour
11. Bristol
12. Afrikaans
13. Birmingham
14. United Nations
15. Four

GEOGRAPHY

ROUND 4

1. Wolverhampton
2. Austria
3. Rome
4. Red Sea
5. North Carolina
6. Greater Manchester
7. Burkina Faso
8. Somalia
9. Wind speed
10. Dublin
11. *The Simpsons*
12. Simoleon
13. Thames
14. Gotham City
15. Saudi Arabia

GEOGRAPHY

ROUND 5

1. Portuguese
2. Anguilla and United States Virgin Islands
3. Canada and US
4. Alcatraz Federal Penitentiary
5. Bahrain
6. Soweto
7. Sutton
8. Egypt
9. Amazon
10. Croydon
11. Maine
12. Sri Lanka
13. Cloud
14. Dakota and Carolina
15. Côte d'Ivoire/Ivory Coast

GEOGRAPHY

ROUND 6

1. Asia, Africa, North America
2. Alabama
3. 1960
4. 12
5. America
6. Edinburgh
7. Summerhouse Estate
8. Dominican Republic
9. Bicester Village
10. Portimão, Portugal
11. Texas
12. Tottenham Court Road Station
13. Missouri
14. Waterloo Station
15. Georgia

GEOGRAPHY

ROUND 7

1. South Africa
2. Tunis
3. Ethiopia
4. Canada
5. Garden of Eden
6. The five pillars of Islam
7. Helvetica
8. West coast
9. Ghana
10. Papiamentu
11. Gambia
12. Swaziland
13. Narnia
14. Paris
15. Netherlands

GEOGRAPHY

ROUND 8

1. The Commonwealth
2. Germany
3. Newham
4. Qatar
5. 'London Bridge'
6. Mexico
7. Texas
8. Uganda and Democratic Republic of the Congo
9. Greek
10. Libya
11. New York
12. Brazil
13. Economic Community of West African States
14. Lion
15. 10 Downing Street

GEOGRAPHY

ROUND 9

1. Atlanta
2. Mastermind
3. Uganda
4. Elizabeth Line
5. Somalia
6. Billingsgate
7. Leicester
8. Seven
9. Dubai
10. Crystal Palace
11. Ireland
12. Jamaica
13. Reading
14. Steven or Stephen
15. Harmattan

GEOGRAPHY

ROUND 10

1. Senegal
2. Ghana
3. 23
4. Ilford
5. Newcastle
6. Grenada
7. Amsterdam
8. Gold
9. New Zealand
10. Sierra Leone
11. Four
12. Italy
13. Manchester
14. Berber (also known as Tamazight)
15. Haringey

GEOGRAPHY

ROUND 11

1. Port-au-Prince
2. LOS
3. Mallard
4. Morocco
5. Liverpool
6. Kenya
7. Islington
8. Benin
9. Senegal
10. 113
11. Mauritian Creole
12. Detroit
13. Jamaica
14. Euro
15. Indonesia

GEOGRAPHY

ROUND 12

1. Algeria
2. Ghana
3. Haiti and Dominican Republic
4. Kenya
5. Africa and Europe
6. Fireboy DML
7. Horn of Africa
8. Diaspora
9. Portuguese
10. Ethiopia
11. All Progressives Congress
12. Mexico
13. Load shedding
14. Nice
15. Nigeria

GEOGRAPHY

ROUND 13

1. Namibia
2. Table Mountain
3. 11
4. Saint Lucia
5. Namib Desert
6. Yoruba
7. Drake
8. Three
9. The Griffins
10. Last/4th
11. Three
12. Jamaica
13. Black Star Square, Accra
14. Six
15. Rome

GEOGRAPHY

ROUND 14

1. Six
2. Ghana
3. Bogotá
4. Louisiana
5. Ashanti
6. Tanzania
7. PALOPs
8. Equatorial Guinea
9. East Africa
10. Georgia
11. Shoreditch
12. Addis Ababa
13. Dominican and Nigerian
14. Westfield Stratford
15. Johannesburg Stock Exchange

GEOGRAPHY

ROUND 15

1. Tunisian dinar
2. Maryland
3. Greece
4. Africa
5. London
6. Turks and Caicos Islands
7. +249
8. Manchester
9. Democratic Republic of the Congo
10. North-west London
11. Somalia
12. Brighton
13. Mali
14. Dutch
15. Harlem

GEOGRAPHY

ROUND 16

1. Africa
2. 0116
3. Islam
4. The Bahamas
5. February
6. Leeds
7. Black Boy Lane
8. KFC
9. Luxford Bar
10. Water taxi or ferry
11. New Orleans
12. Uganda
13. Seychelles
14. CPT
15. Utah

GEOGRAPHY

ROUND 17

1. Sweden
2. Salesforce Tower
3. Coconut cake
4. Canadian
5. Kwacha
6. Manchester
7. City of Westminster
8. Paris
9. 14
10. Trinidad
11. Bristol
12. County of West Midlands
13. Hackney
14. +44
15. ESTA

GEOGRAPHY

ROUND 18

1. Portuguese
2. District and Hammersmith & City
3. Montserrat
4. New York
5. Vienna
6. Alabama and Wyoming
7. Kenya
8. Croydon
9. Mardi Gras
10. Democratic Republic of the Congo
11. Waterloo and Bank
12. Angola
13. 805 Restaurant
14. Brixton
15. Essence Festival

GEOGRAPHY

ROUND 19

1. Ghana
2. Empanada
3. Council estates in London
4. The Bronx
5. Ecuador
6. The Shard
7. Southall
8. Jamaica or Mauritania
9. Southwark
10. Eritrea
11. Zimbabwe
12. Dubai
13. District Line
14. Brazil
15. Crop Over

GEOGRAPHY

ROUND 20

1. Walworth Road
2. Wellington
3. Saint Vincent
4. Brixton
5. Cocoa beans
6. Dutch (Flemish), French and German.
7. +243
8. South Sudan
9. Florida
10. Rabat
11. Victoria Line
12. Asia
13. Sudan
14. South Africa
15. Birmingham

GEOGRAPHY

ROUND 21

1. Belgium
2. Kensington and Chelsea
3. Rwanda
4. Northern Ireland
5. Eight billion
6. Zimbabwe
7. 0151
8. Philadelphia
9. Jamaica
10. Mare Street
11. Germany, Angola and Belgium
12. Tulum
13. Battersea Power Station and Nine Elms
14. Ojuelegba
15. Blackheath

GEOGRAPHY

ROUND 22

1. Birmingham
2. Freetown
3. Jamaica
4. All Saints Road
5. Paraguay
6. St Tropez
7. UGX
8. Brent
9. Algeria and Zimbabwe
10. Algeria, Libya, Mauritania, Morocco, Tunisia
11. Land's End in Cornwall
12. 118
13. Papua New Guinea (840 languages)
14. Park Royal
15. New York

GEOGRAPHY

ROUND 23

1. Saint Lucia
2. Sydenham
3. Alaska
4. Haringey
5. Deptford
6. Newham
7. King's College Hospital
8. Turkey
9. Swahili and English
10. New York
11. Elephant Park
12. North London
13. Kennington
14. Afghanistan
15. Purple

GEOGRAPHY

ROUND 24

1. South America
2. Kensington and Chelsea
3. Vincentian
4. Nakfa
5. Kinshasa
6. Emirati
7. European Union
8. France
9. Canning Town
10. Eritrea
11. Woolwich
12. Bridgetown
13. King's Cross
14. Toronto
15. Oxford Street

POLITICS ROUND

1. Jamaica
2. Wednesday
3. Theresa May
4. Valerie Amos, Baroness Amos
5. 27
6. June 2016
7. Backbenchers
8. Speaker of the House of Commons
9. Frederick Douglass
10. Shirley Chisholm
11. Spelthorne
12. Chauvinism
13. Obi Egbuna, Darcus Howe, Linton Kwesi Johnson, Olive Morris
14. Alternative vote
15. Runnymede Trust

FOOD AND DRINK

ROUND 1

1. Crust
2. Koshari
3. On the rocks
4. Nandocas
5. Crepes and Cones
6. Kosher
7. GAIL's
8. Green bell peppers
9. Genetically modified organism
10. Yeast extract
11. Oreos
12. Type of cheese
13. 2018
14. Pollo
15. Mukbang/meokbang

FOOD AND DRINK

ROUND 2

1. Plantain
2. Sesame seeds
3. Honey
4. Vodka and peach schnapps
5. Halal
6. Yam porridge
7. PERi-Tamer
8. Turmeric
9. 'Live well for less'
10. Michelin star
11. Hard dough bread
12. Doritos
13. Kel Kimble
14. The Arjee Bhajee
15. Red meat

FOOD AND DRINK

ROUND 3

1. Spain
2. Bounty
3. Green bananas
4. Flatbread
5. Pink
6. Soup
7. Ethiopia
8. Cooked
9. Jambalaya
10. Old Kent Road
11. Dates
12. Pescatarian
13. Shot of Prosecco
14. Anejo
15. Fish

FOOD AND DRINK

ROUND 4

1. Daiquiri
2. Brazil
3. Dark Sugars
4. Chickpeas
5. Pepper
6. Butter
7. Bofrot
8. Bagel King
9. Barbados
10. Notting Hill
11. Maize
12. Coconut tart
13. James Cochran
14. Brixton
15. Senegal

EVENTS ROUND

1. Lent
2. Recess
3. 2013
4. Cambridge
5. Festival of Life
6. Natural History Museum
7. Days Like This
8. Ghana Party in the Park
9. Winter Wonderland
10. MTV Video Music Awards (VMAs)
11. Coventry
12. Merky Fest
13. AfroFuture
14. Glastonbury
15. Royal Ascot

MERRY QUIZMAS! ROUND

1. Sorrel
2. John Lewis
3. Mac and cheese
4. 'Can You Stand the Rain'
5. Junkanoo
6. 'O Holy Night'
7. Luke and Matthew
8. Diamond belly ring
9. Melissa's Wardrobe
10. *Bird Box*
11. Kwanzaa
12. Aml Ameen
13. 'Hallelujah'/Alexandra Burke
14. Detty December
15. 'Rudolph the Red-Nosed Reindeer'

ANAGRAMS – ICONIC BLACK AND MIXED BRITISH FOOTBALLERS ROUND

1. Ian Wright
2. Marcus Rashford
3. Rio Ferdinand
4. Sol Campbell
5. Danny Welbeck
6. Ashley Cole
7. Jadon Sancho
8. Jude Bellingham
9. Emile Heskey
10. Theo Walcott
11. Jermain Defoe
12. David James
13. Raheem Sterling
14. Paul Ince
15. Eddie Nketiah

ANAGRAMS – 90S US RAPPERS ROUND

1. Queen Latifah
2. Tupac
3. Method Man
4. Salt-N-Peppa
5. Ice Cube
6. Notorious B.I.G.
7. MC Lyte
8. Black Thought
9. Lil' Kim
10. Mase
11. Lauryn Hill
12. Foxy Brown
13. Snoop Dogg
14. Missy Elliott
15. Lisa Left Eye

ANAGRAMS – CLASSIC GARAGE AND FUNKY SONGS ROUND

1. 'Baby Cakes'
2. 'Sweet Like Chocolate'
3. 'A Little Bit of Luck'
4. '21 Seconds'
5. 'Heartbroken'
6. 'Party Hard'
7. 'Migraine Skank'
8. 'Things We Do for Love'
9. 'On My Mind'
10. 'Movin' Too Fast'
11. 'In the Morning'
12. 'R U Sleeping'
13. 'Little Man'
14. 'No Good 4 Me'
15. 'The Cure & The Cause'

ANAGRAMS – GRIME ARTISTS ROUND

1. Skepta
2. Kano
3. Devilman
4. Stormzy
5. Lady Leshurr
6. AJ Tracey
7. Novelist
8. Flirta D
9. NoLay
10. Ice Kid
11. Lioness
12. P Money
13. D Double E
14. Chip
15. Lisa Maffia

ANAGRAMS – BLACK BRITISH FILMS ROUND

1. *Farming*
2. *Babylon*
3. *Anuvahood*
4. *Bullet Boy*
5. *Rocks*
6. *Shank*
7. *The Intent*
8. *Yardie*
9. *Babymother*
10. *Attack the Block*
11. *Boxing Day*
12. *Pirates*
13. *Blue Story*
14. *The Last Tree*
15. *Kidulthood*

ANAGRAMS – BLACK CARTOON CHARACTERS ROUND

1. Riley Freeman (*The Boondocks*)
2. Penny Proud (*The Proud Family*)
3. Susie Carmichael (*Rugrats*)
4. Cleveland Brown (*Family Guy*)
5. Carl Carlson (*The Simpsons*)
6. Storm (*X-Men*)
7. Trixie Carter (*American Dragon*)
8. Vincent Pierre LaSalle (*Recess*)
9. Gerald Johanssen (*Hey Arnold!*)
10. Numbuh Five (*Codename: Kids Next Door*)
11. Brock (*Pokémon*)
12. Monique (*Kim Possible*)
13. Joe Gardner (*Soul*)
14. Miles Morales (*Spider-Man*)
15. Missy (*Big Mouth*)

ANAGRAMS – REALITY TV ROUND

1. *Big Brother*
2. *Love & Hip Hop*
3. *Married to Medicine*
4. *Basketball Wives*
5. *Bad Girls Club*
6. *Love Is Blind*
7. *Run's House*
8. *Flavor of Love*
9. *RuPaul's Drag Race*
10. *Married at First Sight*
11. *Temptation Island*
12. *Sweet Life*
13. *Peckham's Finest*
14. *Joseline's Cabaret*
15. *America's Next Top Model*

ANAGRAMS – FOOD AND DRINK (DIASPORA FAVOURITES) ROUND

1. Magnum
2. Four wings and chips
3. Bofrot
4. Mac and cheese
5. Jollof rice
6. Supermalt
7. Saltfish fritters
8. Wray & nephew
9. Orange Fanta
10. Beef patty
11. Jerk chicken
12. Plantain
13. Festival
14. Coleslaw
15. Meat pie

ANAGRAMS – BLACK TV SHOWS ROUND

1. *The Boondocks*
2. *The Proud Family*
3. *My Wife and Kids*
4. *All of Us*
5. *Black-ish*
6. *Insecure*
7. *Girlfriends*
8. *Sister, Sister*
9. *Everybody Hates Chris*
10. *Kenan & Kel*
11. *Snowfall*
12. *Being Mary Jane*
13. *Chewing Gum*
14. *Riches*
15. *Greenleaf*

ANAGRAMS – THROWBACK BRANDS ROUND

1. Ed Hardy
2. Pastry
3. Franklin & Marshall
4. True Religion
5. Juicy Couture
6. Avirex
7. New Era
8. Baby Phat
9. Paul's Boutique
10. Star in the Hood
11. Ralph Lauren
12. Evisu
13. Schott NYC
14. G-Star
15. Aqua Master

ANAGRAMS – LATE-20TH-CENTURY TECH ROUND

1. BlackBerry
2. Floppy disk
3. Tamagotchi
4. Walkman
5. Game Boy
6. Projector
7. Infrared
8. VHS player
9. Dial-up
10. Film camera
11. MP3 player
12. Nokia
13. iPod Nano
14. Nintendo DS
15. Flip phone

FILL IN THE BLANKS ROUND

1. It's giving
2. Say less
3. Jawn
4. Charge it
5. Take an 'L'
6. Bredriano
7. Soft life
8. The pressure is getting werser
9. Streets are cold
10. Gone clear
11. Mazza
12. Ghosted
13. Clapped
14. Caught in 4K
15. No cap

BLACK THEATRE WORD SEARCH ROUND

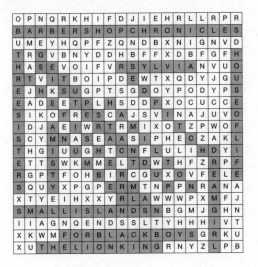

```
O P N Q R K H I F D J I E H R L L R P R
B A R B E R S H O P C H R O N I C L E S
U M E Y H Q P F Z Q N D B X N I G N V D
T R G V B N Y D D H B F F X D B F G F H
H A S E V O I F V R S Y L V I A N V U O
R T V I T B O I P D E W T X Q D Y J G U
E J H K S U G P T S G D O Y P O D Y P S
E A D E E T P L H S D D P X O C U C C E
S I K O F R E S C A J S V I N A J U V O
I D J A E I W R T R M I X O T Z P W O F
S C Y M N A S E A A S I P H E C Z A K L
T H G I U U G H T C N F L U L I H D Y I
E T T S W K M M E L T D W T H F Z R P F
R G P T F O H B I R C G U X O V F E L E
S Q U Y X P G P E R M T N P P N R A N A
X T Y E I H X X Y R L A W W W P X M F J
S M A L L I S L A N D S N B G M J G H N
I I A G N Q E N D S S L T Y H H H I V T
X K W M F O R B L A C K B O Y S G R K U
X U T H E L I O N K I N G R N Y Z L P B
```

POPULAR DANCES WORD SEARCH ROUND

```
C R S X G H L U O C K N D O M B O L O K
Z O S B O X E U R J E Z Y S H A K U I M
M R U F R G C B G L G Q B I P E D N G A
L A F P F A C Q I J Z P C O H T O B A V
L Z X L É O E U A R J Z K D W P U T Z C
Q O L M K D D I T F E H V I T P G N N N
M N X F C S É F Q T W Y P F H B I X A Q
P T M Q Q N F C R J I W G E C H E D E J
H O I C A N D Y A Z H N C V U K P F N L
D T G V G S P P O L P K G F K V A M A V
T U R S F Q T O T A É Y H S E C X A E I
P M A N U J E A X W P K X V H L P S M W
A C I F L P X M N P E P A B U A Q X Q L
X R N I F S E I D K A R Y T F V P G J G
J I E Z D N Y R D V Y A K V S J C E W W
J P S S V M A J M A O L E N G F Z W S S
Z W K E G S O Y K A S R E J V G M E O S
V A A H O R U M B A N T S G N T L A Y J
L L N H J X G I N I A A R G G W A N U M
R K K G T N V Z E X A J U I F V P X U Q
```

TV AND FILM WORD SEARCH ROUND

H	W	P	A	I	D	I	N	F	U	L	L	D	K	G	N	Q	W	H	S
L	N	G	I	R	L	S	T	R	I	P	E	I	U	K	G	F	C	G	V
F	R	U	I	T	V	A	L	E	S	T	A	T	I	O	N	A	O	E	E
B	H	I	D	D	E	N	F	I	G	U	R	E	S	V	I	M	M	Y	S
V	X	V	H	Q	M	N	I	E	C	P	H	V	J	M	X	Y	I	H	P
B	H	M	T	A	T	H	I	N	K	L	I	K	E	A	M	A	N	H	W
L	E	U	J	L	L	H	M	M	X	O	E	C	N	T	W	D	G	E	A
T	B	C	A	E	L	F	E	G	T	L	J	K	X	D	R	J	T	S	V
D	W	V	I	E	J	C	O	W	M	E	Z	N	V	R	N	I	O	D	A
B	T	H	I	T	C	H	X	F	E	W	U	Q	C	O	I	J	A	I	D
H	S	R	D	W	Y	U	W	Q	A	D	B	W	R	C	E	Q	M	T	L
K	G	I	G	X	E	O	K	H	U	Y	D	X	E	K	R	C	E	J	R
E	J	R	S	E	L	D	F	Z	O	A	E	I	W	S	D	C	R	I	O
R	P	U	U	T	T	C	W	G	M	B	U	L	N	R	X	D	I	A	S
C	D	V	L	S	E	O	U	T	O	I	P	B	L	G	Q	K	C	R	I
H	C	Q	L	B	H	R	U	L	U	D	I	M	Z	O	P	P	A	Z	E
I	Y	C	I	L	B	H	A	T	K	R	S	B	F	L	W	A	T	R	N
N	Q	C	W	D	J	N	O	C	D	B	N	Z	S	E	P	S	R	O	J
G	S	L	O	G	X	A	L	U	T	X	K	U	U	V	L	E	U	T	T
H	W	Q	M	W	U	G	I	Z	R	Y	R	A	G	F	B	Q	Y	N	Y

MAP OF THE WORLD

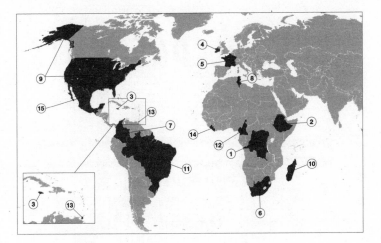

1. Democratic Republic of the Congo
2. Ethiopia
3. Jamaica
4. Ireland
5. France
6. South Africa
7. Colombia
8. Tunisia
9. US
10. Madagascar
11. Brazil
12. Cameroon
13. Trinidad and Tobago
14. Liberia
15. Mexico

ACKNOWLEDGEMENTS

I am eternally grateful and thankful to my family, friends, the PRTYHERE team and community. This wouldn't be possible without you ❤

Love, Sanae

Doris Edobor and Bukola Loko – you are my whole world. My batch > your batch. Thank you <3

Love, Shay